IAN R MITCHELL taught for over 20
gave up teaching to devote himself t
published many titles and won both
Mountain Literature and the Outd___ __
Excellence. He is the author of a standard textbook on Bismarck and
has authored several books on mountaineering, including the classic
Mountain Days and Bothy Nights (with Dave Brown, 1987) and
Scotland's Mountains Before the Mountaineers (1998, rev. edn 2013).
A native of Aberdeen, and author of *Aberdeen Beyond the Granite*
(2010), Ian has lived in Glasgow since 1973, and has written widely
about his adoptive city, most recently *A Glasgow Mosaic: Explorations
Around the City's Urban Icons* (2013).

*A plethora of fascinating historical facts... Mitchell takes
us behind [Glasgow's] facade to unveil some real treasures...
the warmth and wit of working-class Glasgow provides the
book's heart and soul.*
DAILY MAIL on *This City Now*

*Ian Mitchell's infectious enthusiasm for the places visited in
this book leaves the reader with a compelling urge to don
walking shoes and retrace his steps.*
MORNING STAR on *Clydeside, Red, Orange and Green.*

Walking Through Glasgow's Industrial Past

This City Now – and Then

IAN R MITCHELL

Luath Press Limited
EDINBURGH
www.luath.co.uk

First published 2005 as *This City Now*.
This new, revised and updated edition published 2015

ISBN: 978-1-910021-15-6

Extracts from Edwin Morgan's poem *King Billy*
from *New Selected Poems* (2000), and from Hugh MacDiarmid's
poems *Second Hymn to Lenin, Third Hymn to Lenin* and
A Drunk Man Looks at the Thistle from *Complete Poems* (1993),
reproduced by kind permission of Carcanet Press Limited.

Extracts from Dorothy Paul's *Dorothy:
Revelations of a Rejected Soprano* and John Cairney's
East End to West End: First Steps in an Autobiographical Journey
reproduced by kind permission of Mainstream Publishing/Random House.

Extracts from Ralph Glasser's *Growing Up in the Gorbals*
reproduced by kind permission of Pan MacMillan.

The paper used in this book is recyclable. It is made from
low chlorine pulps produced in a low energy, low emissions manner from
renewable forests.

Printed and bound by
Bell & Bain Ltd., Glasgow

Maps © Jim Lewis, 2015

Typeset in 10.5 point Sabon
by 3btype.com

To Mungo's Bairns

Spirit of Lenin, light on this city now!
Light up this city now!

HUGH MacDIARMID, 'Third Hymn to Lenin'

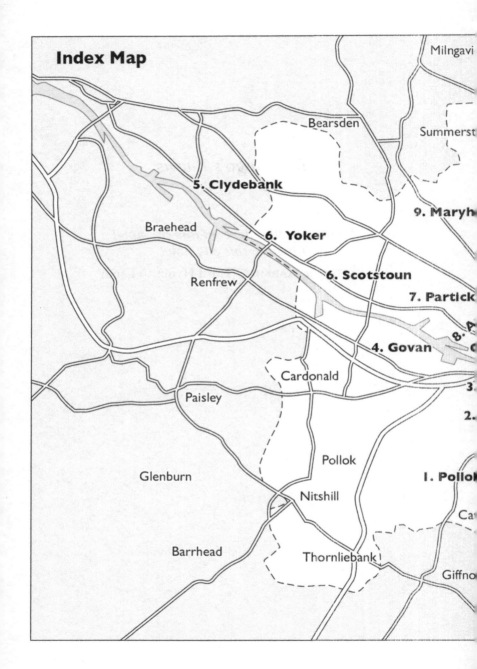

Index Map

Milngavi

Bearsden

Summerst

5. Clydebank

9. Maryh

Braehead

6. Yoker

6. Scotstoun

Renfrew

7. Partick

8.

4. Govan

Cardonald

3.

Paisley

2.

Pollok

Glenburn

1. Pollok

Nitshill

Ca

Barrhead

Thornliebank

Giffno

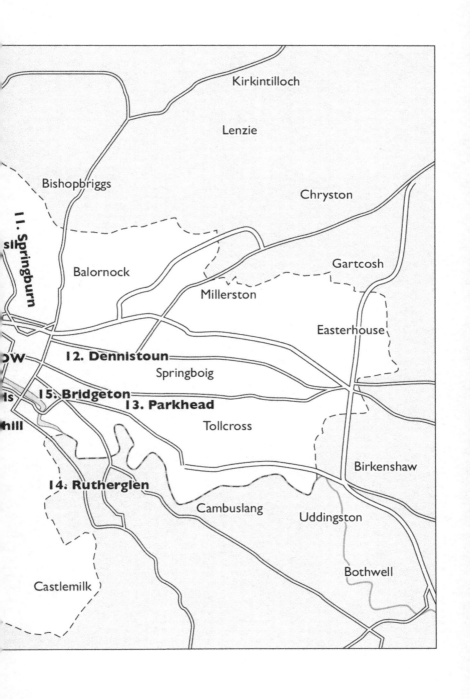

Contents

Foreword to the 2015 Edition

This City Now... and Then

AS A WRITER I have two passions that inform and inspire my work: mountains and cities. Unlike mountains, cities do not stand still and this is very true of Glasgow in the ten years since I wrote *This City Now*, published in 2005. In that decade it has become evident that the book has become *This City Then*, and is in need of a thorough reworking.

In this new edition I have taken the opportunity to update the book as regards the physical and social developments that have taken place in the various areas covered. I have also sought to infill any omissions from the previous version, and to correct any errors I have discovered or which readers have been kind enough to point out to me.

The decade has been one of kaleidoscopic change for the city, with its profile being increasingly raised and its achievements recognised at a wider level. One can mention it being awarded the Glasgow City of Music title by UNESCO, Pollok Park being named Best Park in Britain in 2007 and Europe's Best Park in 2008, or the Riverside Museum being chosen as European Museum of the Year in 2013. The Academy of Urbanism named Glasgow European City of the Year in 2011 and has twice (with the Merchant City and the West End) granted the title of Neighbourhood of the Year to areas of Glasgow, albeit not ones which feature in this book. The 2014 Commonwealth Games both recognised and raised the status of the city internationally. Though not yet universally acknowledged as the first Second City in Europe in social and cultural terms, a status that I have elsewhere claimed for it, Glasgow is on its way in that respect.

Over the last ten years there has been a marked improvement in the appearance and condition of much of the built fabric of a city that increasingly depends on its past to underwrite its present, and recognises this fact. Thirty years ago, the idea of tourism as Glasgow's second industry would have seemed mad; today it is a fact. Change has been uneven it the city, though. There are some areas which have been much improved, largely for the benefit of the inhabitants, but some which have changed more as a process of gentrification and social cleansing. There are some districts wherein little has changed in ten years, while some others have been transformed almost beyond recognition, either socially or architecturally, during the same timeframe. Regrettably, due to a general increase in poverty in the city in the last five years, there are some areas of Glasgow which have declined further into ghettoisation and marginalisation since this book was first published.

The reasons for this are obvious. In the first place the economic crisis unleashed in 2008 by the collapse of the banking system has put into reverse many of the minimal gains previously made in the fight against poverty. And year on year the madness of the attempt to manufacture a counterfeit property-owning democracy through home ownership is leading to an increase in homelessness and a marked decrease in the quality of the private housing stock in certain areas. The ending of the Right to Buy social housing scheme and the increase in the rented social housing stock can help in this regard.

There is only limited scope for Glasgow City Council to counter these tendencies, but one thing that would help is the gaining of metropolitan status for Glasgow and the extension of the city's boundaries to include its contiguous areas and dormitory towns. Contrary to the stereotyped image of it as a parasitic city with its population living on benefits, Glasgow gives more, much more, to the rest of the Scottish and UK economy than it gets back financially. Glasgow's contribution to Scotland's business rates pool is much greater than it in turn receives back: it is subsidising the rest of Scotland in that regard. It is also subsidising the leafy suburbs that surround it: 50 per cent of Glasgow's workplaces are occupied by these people, and their wages go outwith the city to be spent. The increase in revenue the city would gain from including within its boundaries the rich suburbs – and their council tax base – would be one step in the right direction. I have suggested that Clydebank and Rutherglen should be part of Glasgow; so too should East Dunbartonshire and East Renfrewshire, two of the richest parts of Scotland. This would create a city of about one million people, which would be able to deal better with its social problems than at present, and would also be a much bigger hitter for its interests on the national and international stage.

In his book *The Tenement: A Way of Life* (1979), Frank Worsdall suggested that Glasgow was, 'a city of desolation, devoid of [the] community spirit which used to be so strong, but above all a city devoid of pride'. Worsdall was a man who did much in the campaign against the wanton destruction of Glasgow's built heritage, seeing the link between physical environment and community, and his impact has been great and beneficial. But I doubt that his picture of a Glasgow devoid of community spirit and pride was true then, and it is certainly not true three-and-a-half decades later.

Attitudes as well as buildings have improved in the last decade or more, as the incredible success of the initially modest Doors Open Day shows. Started as a minor event where one could see inside certain iconic Glasgow buildings, it has grown into a major weeklong festival with associated walks and talks. The great improvement in facilities, such as walking and cycle tracks, and the publication by the City Council – and other organisations – of a whole stream of heritage trails is also testimony to an increased interest, and pride, in Glasgow's history and heritage. When I initially wrote this book, I hoped it would encourage the more adventurous to explore what might be termed the more abrasive areas of the city, though I realised that for most readers the book would represent an armchair journey only. But people are increasingly to be found wandering in Govan, Bridgeton and the other areas described in this book, and some have noted – and remarked to me – that wandering about with fingers and thumbs in various pages was a nuisance. I have therefore summarized 'Suggested Walks' at the end of each chapter so that, after reading, the explorer has a helpful *précis* to follow.

The aim of this book, as with the other urban works I have written, is not only to inform and interest readers and potential explorers, but to raise the profile of areas that are in danger of being forgotten as more salubrious parts of Glasgow receive all the attention – areas often dismissed as being of little interest and with little worth saving. Also, I have given myself the role of Old Mortality of the working class, trying to help keep alive the memory of the martyrs who in the past fought for a better society. They lost their battle, that cannot be denied, but an updated version of their message and ideals is increasingly important in a world that appears, lemming-like, to be wedded to a now twice-failed philosophy of free-marketeering that is leading us, not into the 21st century, but back to the worst excesses of the 19th.

Ian R Mitchell
April 2015

INTRODUCTION

Glasgow Despite Them

AS MOUNTAINS CAN be seen as the supreme work of nature, so is the city the greatest work of human geology, the high point of social and cultural evolution. For the Greeks and Romans the *polis* was the social ideal and the citizen its representative. For the early and later Christians, Heaven was a city, and in the Renaissance the city-state embodied the humanistic strivings of the era. For the Victorians too, despite the development of rural romanticism, civic pride was a central driving force in their achievements.

A great city (the Germans use the term *Weltstadt*) is qualitatively different from a small one: a critical mass is needed to transform the parochial into the cosmopolitan – though other things are needed too. Not every big city is a *Weltstadt*, indeed most are not. A *Weltstadt* is one which has had a clear impact on world history, and where the main issues of its epoch – intellectual, social and political – have been posed. James Watt's invention here of the steam engine and the launching of the industrialisation and urbanisation of the Western world alone would make Glasgow a *Weltstadt*. But we should not forget that, though now small on the city scale, at the beginning of the 20th century, when it produced two British Prime Ministers (Bonar Law and Campbell-Bannerman), Glasgow was in the top ten metropolises in Europe. Over one million people then lived in the Second City of the Empire. The former Second City may now only be fourth in the United Kingdom after Birmingham and Manchester; but they were never world cities. Edinburgh, however, was – though that was back in the 18th century.

I appreciated Glasgow – though not uncritically – before it was Miles Better. I moved here over 40 years ago when it appeared as if the city was dying. Deindustrialisation had begun, as had depopulation. The city had a very negative image and even amongst its own population low civic esteem was prevalent. The buildings were still being indiscriminately flattened and I recall that there were only a handful of them being stone-cleaned and restored. The architecture (mainly in its Victorian expressions) fascinated me. The city's skyline against the ever-varying cloud patterns of its dominant southwesterlies created

drama that constantly drew me onto the city street. I grew to appreci-
ate the blue-black sky against the multistorey blocks of the Red Road,
dawn emerging behind the Necropolis in winter, and Park Circus
glowing on a summer's evening, as much as I did a Cuillin sunset, or
morning on the winter plateau of the Cairngorms.

The culture of Glasgow also attracted me, and not just in the
availability of theatre and art, things belatedly recognised when
Glasgow became European City of Culture in 1990 and City of
Architecture in 1999. Glasgow is probably the only place in Britain
where, even imperfectly, there is a working-class cultural dominance,
which constantly refers back to itself and its own history rather than
to the rural hinterland of its origins, as the working-class culture
of Aberdeen, for example, tends to do. This is not to exaggerate
and elevate the consciousness of the Glasgow workers to something greater than it is or was, but still this is a city dominated by
its working class and the history of their organisations and struggles. Often this is forgotten and sterrheid schmaltz is passed off as
Glasgow working-class culture.

'The glory of Glasgow is in what the unknown working-class districts contain,' said James Hamilton Muir in *Glasgow in 1901*, written
to mark the Empire Exhibition of that year, when the city was at its
apogee. Although that book did not quite live up to its promise of
revealing these glories, I take its comment as my starting point.

Walking Through Glasgow's Industrial Past looks at the development of some of the main working-class areas of Glasgow from their
origins till the time when Glasgow was a world city, and follows their
subsequent evolution. Most of these areas were independent communities, swallowed up by Glasgow's growth and to some extent left
behind by its decline, and to the familiar pattern of inner-city decay.
Most, too, still retain their local identities. I have chosen areas that
have a story to tell in relation to the history of the Glasgow working
class; its industries, struggles, organisations and notable personalities.
In addition I am convinced that the social significance of areas like
Govan, Bridgeton and Springburn, along with the other inner-city
districts treated in this work, is in many cases matched by their little-
known historical and architectural heritage.

The experience of urban rambling is sadly underrated, and mainly
limited to the obvious tourist cities. This was not always the case:
before 1950, exploration in our industrial cities was more widespread.
In Glasgow, for example, there are many books from half a century

ago and more, giving its inhabitants tips about, and guides to, places to walk. James Cowan's *From Glasgow's Treasure Chest* (1933) is an example of a genre that goes back at least to John Tweed's *Guide to Glasgow and the Clyde* of 1872. However, the rise of the motor car – and possibly the decline of civic pride in our industrial cities which have undergone painful transformation in the last half century as industry and population moved out – seemed to have all but killed off this tradition of urban walking, and writing about urban walking. With the urban renaissance going on around us in our increasingly post-industrial cities, including Glasgow, there are signs of a welcome reinvention of this tradition.

Glasgow, like many big cities, resembles a series of medium-sized towns, whose inhabitants overlap in the city centre, or in places such as football grounds. Even more so in the days when industries were identified with areas, and inhabitants of specific areas tended to work locally. This multiplicity of apparent parochialisms is overlain, however, with a very strong sense of city identity. Whether from Park-head or Partick, the ruling motto is 'Glasgow belongs to me' – and there are no no-go areas for the Glasgow working class. In Edinburgh, on the other hand, the city centre belongs to the middle classes and to the tourists, the working class remaining ghettoed in the outer districts. I recall being in Rogano's, one of Glasgow's top restaurants, when a punter entered, and, on discovering the establishment did not sell Tennents lager, left, but with the dismissive comment to the waiter that 'Ye could dae wi a band in here, son, tae liven things up'. The restaurant was at fault, not him.

Dr Johnson, when he visited Scotland in the mid-18th century, said that most Scots knew as little of the Highlands as they did of Borneo. The same might be said today about Glasgow, not only of Glasgow's increasing tourist traffic, but of many of its own inhabitants – especially its suburban ones. They may well be familiar with the West End, or the city centre and Merchant City, but with little else. The city limits are the new Borneo, ignored, or driven through at speed. Johnson also said of the Highlanders, 'All they have left is their language and their poverty,' and many might be tempted to repeat this of Govan or Bridgeton today. It was not true for the Highlanders 200 years ago, but Johnson's intellectual limitations prevented him seeing this, and neither is it true for the inhabitants of Glasgow's Victorian and Edwardian industrial areas today. TC Smout, a historian I admire, could print a photograph of Ibrox Stadium in 1921 in his *Century of the Scottish People*, and caption it 'Ibrox in its Urban Desert'. One would have to enquire what Smout knew of Govan when he wrote this. He was clearly ignorant of Govan's Gaelic Choir, its 250-year-old Govan Fair, or its unique collection of incised medieval sculpture in Govan Old Kirk. Govan, or Bridgeton, or Springburn – all these working-class areas had choirs, clubs, bands, societies and a richer cultural life, one would say without hesitation, than many a suburban development.

Finding this world can be adventurous. While much can be assimilated from reading, it is by wandering around on foot you get a feel for a place. Walter Benjamin wrote of his urban rambles in inter-war Paris that he was 'botanising the asphalt'. I see my urban walking as 'politicising the pavements'. There is an undeniable edge to walking in Glasgow because of the proximity of different social classes in certain borderlands. There are places where you can turn left or right from pub, shop, café – even a tenement close – and find yourself in a seemingly different world. In one direction you can be somewhere where apartments cost £500,000 and in another direction, within a few steps, nothing seems to cost more than £1. Redevelopment has created areas where the two worlds are intermingled, without apparently fusing, as for example in Calton. It is in areas like this that you realise the accuracy of what Baudelaire, a dedicated urban walker, said: 'What are the dangers of the forest and the prairie compared with the daily shocks and conflicts of civilisation?' In an age of increasing painting-by-numbers travel, the urban edge has a claim to being one of the remaining frontiers.

In most areas though, urban geography separates, rather than mingles, social classes. Walking about, you see how urban planners and consumer 'choice' have largely segregated working-class from middle-class areas by a series of rivers, canals, railways (hence the phrase 'wrong side of the tracks') and larger roads, almost as complete as any apartheid. Parks also tend to enforce social segregation, establishing an acceptable physical distance between high- and low-income social groups. Working-class areas, however, tend to flow more into one another, do not tend to be so brutally divided from each other as they are from the middle-class areas, but pounding the asphalt you soon realise that districts that appear to coalesce are sharply defined, in a way that driving or going by bus does not reveal.

The identity of specific areas is created in many ways. Of course, there is the labeling established by libraries, post offices, street names, names of parks and schools, which tells you that you are in Govan or Gorbals. Wall murals and gang slogans are another way of defining territory. People meeting in cafés, pubs and shops define a geosocial nexus, as did, in the past, local workplaces. The physical and the mental combine to produce definite *quartiers*. People know where they are. Everyone will tell you that the railway at Bellgrove station divides Dennistoun from the Gallowgate. I stood on one side of the road photographing the high flats of Pollokshaws on the other, and was informed by someone that where I was standing wasn't the Shaws – though I was only across the road from what I photographed. At meetings I attended over the restoration of Maryhill Burgh Halls, the locals discoursed intensely over not only what was Maryhill, but of the boundaries of its subdivisions, Gairbraid, Wyndford and Cadder.

I have been discovering this city for 40 years. William Faulkner, the Mississippi novelist, said he would never exhaust his postage stamp of southern soil; I feel it would take several lifetimes to exhaust Glasgow, which still surprises, amazes, delights and angers in turn. These are all emotions I would wish to hold on to and which are stimulated by residence here.

In 1951 Glasgow (or 'The Dear Green Place,' according to a possible translation of its original Gaelic name of Cathures) still had over a million people. Since the 1960s Glasgow has hemorrhaged population: today there are around 600,000 inhabitants. Over a period of four decades Glasgow has lost population at a rate of almost 10,000 a year. Put another way, that means that in each decade since 1970, Glasgow lost more of its population than the entire Highlands during the Clearances of the 18th and 19th centuries. There are signs, however, that this fall is bottoming out: 2003 was the first year for over three decades in which the city's population did not decline.[1] We get volumes of poetry about the Highland Clearances; but where are the sonnets to the silent stones of Springburn? True, the population of Springburn or Govan or Bridgeton was not forced onto boats and didn't have their roofs burned over their heads, but for most there was no alternative to leaving. If all had stayed, today Glasgow's unemployment rate would be on the levels of Calcutta or Cairo.

Much of the skilled working class was forced to leave the city to find work in other parts of Scotland or abroad, but much of the upper and middle classes left by choice. Unwilling to pay Glasgow's rates, and later council tax, and unwilling to have their children mix with Mungo's bairns, these people moved out to the suburbs, through still parasiting on the city. Half of Glasgow's working population live outwith the city boundaries, many are actually employed by the City Council, and these middle classes are disproportionate users of the city's cultural and other facilities. Today Glasgow is a city of lower professionals such as teachers, social workers and other intellectual and cultural workers, and of unskilled workers and the increasingly hereditary underclass. Its industrial base has declined to about 30,000 employees and its industrial glory has gone forever. It is a Naples of the North.

Despite being abandoned by its own bourgeoisie and middle class (with the exception of its intellectual sector, which embraces working-class cultural and political values to a great extent), and despite the machinations of the Edinburgh establishment in issues like boundary revisions, Glasgow has come through a period of economic decline alive and moderately kicking. Glasgow may not have flourished, but it has survived – despite them, and at least in part because of the resilience bred of its working-class culture. I said previously that the silent stones of Springburn have not inspired any sonnets, but they and the others of this city have inspired this book. I hope it will light up this city now, and open many eyes to its limitless and unending fascination.

---

1 Note to the 2015 Edition
  This trend has continued. The census of 2011 showed the first rise in Glasgow's population since 1951, of about 25,000 people, half of whom were immigrants to what has always been a city of immigrants. However, the main strategy to be pursued to increasing the city's resident population should be that of incorporating the contiguous urban districts in a Metropolitan Glasgow.

CHAPTER ONE

John Maclean's Pollokshaws

ON 1 DECEMBER 1923, 5,000 people marched four miles south from Eglinton Toll in Glasgow to Eastwood cemetery, passing through the district of Pollokshaws. Possibly the most loved – and probably also the most hated – man in Scotland, John Maclean, had died. Another 10,000 lined the streets to pay tribute to a person whose life ended prematurely at 44 from overwork, the effects of imprisonment and – eventually – from near-starvation. Fifty years thereafter, in 1973, a memorial was erected near the Old Town House of Pollokshaws, to the district's most famous son, which stated simply:

In Memory of John Maclean

Born in Pollokshaws on 24 August 1879

Died 30 November 1923

Famous pioneer of working class education he forged the
Scottish link in the golden chain of world socialism.

When Maclean was born, Pollokshaws was a village, though an expanding one, still outwith Glasgow's city boundaries: in fact it was

John MacLean's funeral, 1923: This picture shows part of the huge crowd that gathered to pay their respects to Maclean. The coffin is leaving Auldhouse Road and one of the pallbearers was James Maxton.

Pollokshaws

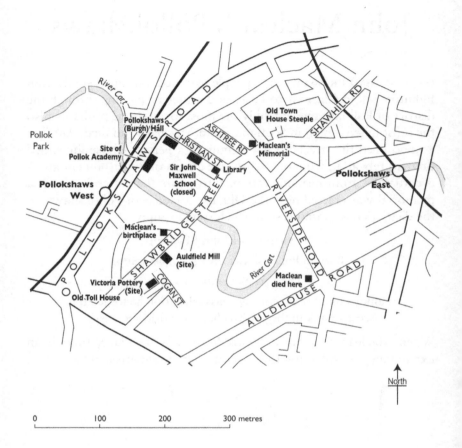

Pollokshaws Route Summary

1 Take a train to Pollokshaws West.

2 Walk down Pollokshaws Road to the Round Toll.

3 Walk up Shawbridge Street to Christian Street (Sir John Maxwell Primary School and the Burgh Hall).

4 Proceed past the library to the Maclean memorial and the Old Town House.

5 Walk up Shawhill Road to the four multi-storey flats to take in the fine view, before heading to Pollokshaws East station, or go back to Pollokshaws Road, to Pollok Country Park (The Burrell Collection, Pollok House).

Approximate route time: 1.5 hours

in the Eastwood district of Renfrewshire. Though its origins go back to medieval times, it began to assume importance in the later 18th century as a textile-weaving town, using the waterpower of the River Cart and its subsidiary, the Auldhouse Burn. By the mid-19th century, several weaving factories had been established in the village as well as print and dye works, the Auldhouse and Cart often running red with the dyes poured into them. It was never a classic tenement area, but a mix of pre- and post-industrial and semirural buildings, many of which were in worse condition than the tenements of areas like Govan and Bridgeton.

The main landed family in this area were the Maxwells of Pollok, whose mansion house lay in what is now Pollok Park to the west of 'the Shaws'. Though landed proprietors, the Maxwells, like many others of their class, eventually became more dependent on their industrial than their agricultural wealth, and they opened or leased many coal mines on their lands and took an active part in developing the textile industries of Pollokshaws itself. When Maclean was born the Maxwells still wielded enormous power in the burgh as employers, kirk patrons and as office-bearers on the burgh council and its various agencies. This only really began to decline when the Shaws was annexed to Glasgow in 1912. The Maxwell family on their adjoining estate lived on almost exactly the same amount of land as was occupied by the 12,000 people of the Shaws: such was the wealth

gap in Victorian Britain. Incidentally, Maclean approved of the annexation of the Shaws by Glasgow. Indeed, one of his constant political
demands was the extension of the city boundaries to include its contiguous urban areas: a demand as relevant today as it was 100 years ago.

Maclean was born at 59 King Street, just south of the Shawbrig
over the Cart, and a street now subsumed by Shawbridge Road. His
parents were both immigrants to Pollokshaws, and both victims of the
process of clearance and famine that drove many Highlanders to come
to Glasgow in the mid-19th century. His father, Daniel, was a potter
who came to Glasgow from Mull, after a spell working at Bo'ness. He
worked in the Victoria Pottery of Lockhart and Sons in Cogan Street,
a couple of minutes walk from King Street: the works opened in 1855
and finally closed in 1952. Daniel died in 1888 from silicosis ('potter's
lung'). The Victoria Pottery occupied the land now given over to the
car park of the Auldhouse Retail Park.

Daniel's death left John's mother, Anne, to look after four children. Anne had married Daniel at the nearby mining village of Nitshill
in 1867. As a child Anne had walked with her mother, neither speaking a word of English, from Corpach (near Fort William) to join her
own father working as a quarryman in Paisley. She had been a weaver
before marriage and resumed this trade as a widow at the Auldfield
Mill, which lay just across the road in Cogan Street from where her
husband Daniel had worked. The mill was opened by John Cogan in
1851, and occupied the present vacant lot next to the Comet store car
park. The village character of the Shaws at this time was emphasised
by the fact that the Macleans' Church, the Original Secession Church,
lay just round the corner from Cogan Street, in Shawbridge Street.
The building is presently the parish kirk of Pollokshaws. The Shaws
was a small world in those days, with the part south of the Shawbrig
where the Macleans lived, worked and prayed being almost a village
within a village.

Religion played a far greater part in Victorian working-class life
than it subsequently has, and in the Shaws there were ten churches,
a Catholic one, and the others representing every variety of Protestant denomination: Established Kirk, Free Kirk, various Secession
Churches and even a Methodist chapel. The 1895 street map of the
burgh also shows a dozen public houses in the short stretch between
the Old Town House and the Shawbrig, and the pub was the other
pole of working-class life to the kirk in the years before 1900.
Maclean was to become a fierce opponent both of religion and of

alcohol (though he was never a campaigning teetotaler, seeing drunkenness as the result, not the cause, of working-class misery). He looked to provide the working man with better fare for mind and body – working-class education in Marxist political and economic principles – and Maclean spent his free time not in the kirk or the pub but in Pollokshaws Public Library. Though his boyhood Calvinism lapsed, his associated belief in the overriding importance of education never waned. Calvinists believed a study of the Bible must lead to God; with equal fervour Maclean believed the study of Marx must lead to socialism. Maclean is often portrayed as a violent revolutionary. In fact he believed that Marxist education would eventually lead to a peaceful triumph for socialism at the ballot box, and that violence need only be used in self-defence.

Maclean's own education was interesting. He first attended Pollok Academy, which had been established as an elementary school through the efforts of the Burgh council and Sir John Maxwell, 8th Bart. This was built in 1856 and was part designed by Alexander 'Greek' Thomson. It lay on Pollokshaws Road, just opposite the present entrance to Pollok Park, on the presently vacant site south of the Burgh Hall. It was later converted to a secondary school, and eventually demolished in the 1960s. This school was again only a couple of minutes from the Macleans' King Street home – though for his secondary education John had to leave the Shaws and go to Queens Park Secondary. But this did not end his connection with the schools and schoolmasters of Pollokshaws.

Maclean undertook his teacher's training at the Free Kirk Seminary at Trinity in Glasgow's Park Circus area from 1898–1900; he walked from the Shaws to Trinity every day, a round distance of ten miles. Later he did his MA via evening classes at Glasgow University, again using shanks' pony, apparently in a deliberate attempt to maintain his fitness, as well as to save cash. His father's death and his brother's developing tuberculosis had a deep effect on him. He worked as a message boy for various shops in the Shaws and also as a caddie on the nearby Thornliebank Golf Course, which doubtless developed his pedestrian abilities, as did his postie round on student holidays. Maclean was a typical lapsed Calvinist in that he could not be idle; he always had to be doing something. On the few short holidays he took in his life, he usually fretted to return to his propaganda work in Glasgow.

Subsequent to his father's death, followed by the marriage of his sisters and his brother's emigration to South Africa, Maclean moved with his mother to Low Cartcraigs in the Shaws. This was a small cluster of pre-industrial housing and workshops, such as a smiddy, which lay across Pollokshaws Road (between the road and the railway) from the Old Toll House. Anne had given up work in the mill, and took in a lodger as well as having John's earnings once he became a teacher.

Low Cartcraigs is now occupied by the western portion of the Pollokshaws Road dual carriageway, but the Old Toll House dating from around 1800 still stands. It was occupied as a dwelling house till the late 1950s. It lost its original function with the abolition of road tolls and became a public house, serving the horse races, which were held nearby till 1838. These races led to a poem from a mother warning her son against temptation:

Said she, 'Ye may be trod to death
Beneath the horses' paws
And mind ye, lad, the sayin's true
There's queer folk i' the Shaws.'

Many of the good folk of the Shaws around 1900 would probably have recalled that saying as their village was assailed by the preaching of a new set of queer folk – the socialists. Indeed, Maclean's conversion to socialism took place largely within the intellectual structures of his native Shaws – and surprisingly active and varied these were, too.

In 1900 Maclean joined the Progressive Union in Pollokshaws, an organisation that discussed issues such as socialism, anarchism, the natural sciences and social problems generally. Its main aim was the criticism of organised religion, and its members attacked the churches and their teachings at open-air meetings on Sunday afternoons. It is difficult for us to imagine the street culture of politics a century ago: with little bar kirk and pub to entertain them, people flocked to open-air meetings of religious revivalists, temperance campaigners and political agitators, often for the entertainment value. The two most popular open-air stances in the Shaws were Shawbrig itself and the Old Town House, whose steeple still remains today. Hundreds came to listen and to heckle at these meetings. These meetings were covered in the *Pollokshaws News*, which reported in 1901 that Maclean had said socialism would reduce drunkenness, 'and the diminution of drunkenness would result in the diminution of crime'. A lively correspondence ensued from these coverages, to which Maclean himself contributed. Friend and foe alike agreed that Maclean was an electrifying speaker.

The Labour Representation Committee (LRC – soon to become the Labour Party) had just been formed as a federation of trades unions, Co-ops and socialist organisations. The most left wing of the latter was the Social Democratic Federation (SDF), which was avowedly Marxist and which Maclean joined in 1903, setting up the Pollokshaws branch at an open-air meeting outside the Old Burgh Hall in 1906. Local members established a broadsheet, *The Pollokshaws Review*, which was widely distributed, and also distributed leaflets and held many street corner meetings. The branch had about 100 members: 'Not bad for a small town,' commented Maclean. Lecturers from outside were invited, speaking at the new Burgh Hall, the pride of the Shaws, designed by Rowand Anderson and erected in 1898. Here, too, Maclean and the SDF would gather to hear the results of their participation in local elections, which were generally disappointing. The SDF won no council seats in the Shaws or in Glasgow, though the more moderate Independent Labour Party did, preparing the way for its staggering success of gaining ten of Glasgow's 15 parliamentary seats in 1922, with 51 per cent of all votes cast.

Greater success was had, however, by the SDF with the rapidly expanding Co-operative movement. Pollokshaws Co-op lay just south of the present library in Shawbridge Road, and more or less over the dyke of the Sir John Maxwell School – again emphasising the 'village' character of the Shaws at this time. Maclean was an active member of the Pollokshaws Co-operative Society and like others of the SDF argued for a more socialist orientation in the organisation, and he gave lectures to members organised by the Co-operative Educational Committee. Maclean was also elected to represent the Shaws at the national Co-op conference in 1905. Another area of activity was the Eastwood School Board, for which the SDF stood candidates demanding radical education reforms, and where two SDF members were elected in 1908–9. The SDF members called for free, non-denominational education, the raising of the school leaving age to 16 and bursaries for further education.

Maclean and his comrades were also involved in the industrial disputes of the time. One of these took place in the village of Neilston, at the thread mills, where hundreds of girls struck for better wages and a trades union. Some of them lived in the village of Nitshill near the Shaws, and they contacted Maclean and his associates, who gave the girls their support. A march was organised from Neilston to the manager's house at Pollokshields in Glasgow, carrying effigies of the manager to be burnt. One participant recalled:

> Maclean was equal to anything of this kind. He was full of fun and chaff, and so took the hearts of the girls that they would have done anything for him.

> The march with a great banging of tin cans and shouting and singing pursued its noisy way from Neilston to Pollokshields, where the respectable inhabitants were thoroughly disturbed. The meeting was held in a field adjacent to the manager's house. The wage demands were won. The whole of the girls in the factory were organised.

As a schoolteacher Maclean worked in various parts of the South Side of Glasgow; in Polmadie, in Strathbungo and in Kinning Park, but he also taught in Pollokshaws. In 1854, Sir John Maxwell, 8th Bart, had set up an industrial school in the village, training boys for useful trades. This was rebuilt in a new site at Christian Street in 1907 by a partnership between the Burgh council and Sir John Maxwell, 10th Bart – and the school was named after him. The SDF members of the School Board proposed, and got, Maclean a night school job at the John Maxwell School.

From 1908 to 1915 (when he was sacked by the School Board from his day and evening classes for his agitation against the First World War), Maclean taught industrial history and economics to classes of industrial workers, using Karl Marx's *Capital* as the main textbook. Hundreds of workers passed through these classes, their fees paid by their trade unions or by local authority grants. The school continued to operate for many decades as the Shaws primary, and as my son attended it, I often had cause to be there. Maclean's classes must have been held in the gymnasium, as no classroom would have been big enough for the numbers attending.

Many of the shop stewards who attended Maclean's classes became prominent in the industrial unrest (Red Clydeside) during and after the First World War. What is astonishing is that the East-wood School Board initially paid Maclean to give these classes, and that Sir John Maxwell himself was a member of the board. The village atmosphere of the Shaws at this time is further emphasised by the fact that one of Maclean's assistants at his evening classes was another Shaws boy whom he had converted to socialism, James Maxton (later MP for Bridgeton 1922–46). Maxton's own father had taught at Pollok Academy when Maclean was a pupil.

Large numbers who attended the Marxist evening classes came from the huge new industrial complex of Weir's of Cathcart, with which Maclean had an especial connection, as it lay near to the Shaws. He gave many factory gate meetings at Weir's during strikes before and after 1914, at a time when his influence was at its greatest and his political clarity at its sharpest. William (later Lord) Weir's role with the Ministry of Munitions made him an especial target for Maclean. The latter was delighted when in 1915 the first significant strike during the war broke out at the Cathcart plant, when 2,000 men downed tools. From then until the defeat of the 40-hour strike in 1919, Weir's was one of the bastions of Clydeside militancy. William Weir's attitude to the strikes was outraged jingoism, and he fulminated that 'nothing other than martial law in the munitions districts will solve our troubles and difficulties'.

From day one, Maclean denounced the war as an imperialist one and called for the workers of all countries to take action against it. This tireless message earned him both praise from Lenin and spells of imprisonment. His words from the dock in May 1918 still thrill: 'I am here, then, not as the accused,' he stated, 'I am here as the accuser of capitalism dripping with blood from head to foot'. Before this, 100,000 Clydeside workers had struck on 1 May 1918, demanding an end to the war, and the May Day procession was rerouted past Duke Street Jail where Maclean awaited trial. The marchers chanted John's name so that he could hear even within his cell. Weir's is one of the few industrial plants from that Red Clydeside period still working today, employing about 600 workers, though it is no longer part of the Weir's industrial conglomerate.

In 1909 Maclean had married Agnes Wood and moved to Langside, to the east of Pollokshaws. His increasingly national political profile, and then his opposition to the First World War resulting in periods of imprisonment, took him away from the Shaws. The toleration shown by the political establishment to Maclean and his views rapidly evaporated when war was declared, and he was soon fired from his teaching job. These strains led to the breakdown of his marriage. Though his wife was not overtly hostile to Maclean's politics, her family was, and she herself was not politically engaged. On his release from prison he returned to Pollokshaws, and took rooms at 42 Auldhouse Road, a short distance from where he was born, and within sight, across the River Cart, of the factories where his parents had laboured. He was hoping that this would be a base for reconciliation with his wife, and he had the place redecorated with money he could scarcely afford, hoping vainly that he might be re-employed in a teaching post.

He kept up his frenzied level of political activity, but his health had been seriously sapped by his spells in prison. Also he relied on pamphlet sales and collections at meetings to maintain himself; with the onset of the postwar slump these sources of income dried up, and at the end Maclean was apparently living on a diet of oatmeal and dates. Characteristically, at a time when he was giving debilitating outdoor winter lectures, he gifted his only overcoat to an immigrant from Barbados, Neil Johnston, whom he had given shelter to in his house. From 42 Auldhouse Road, Maclean took his last earthly trip to Eastwood cemetery. James Maxton was one of the pallbearers.

And what of the Shaws? Even in 1955, 77 per cent of the population of Pollokshaws lived in one or two rooms, 89 per cent had no bath and 83 per cent of the housing was classed as substandard. The area was comprehensively flattened thereafter, leaving only a few public buildings, and replaced by 12 multistorey blocks of flats. The Old Stag Inn – located behind the Town House Steeple, all that remains of the former seat of local government – identifies one of the few tenements still standing in the area. Almost all of the industry in the Shaws closed down and its former sites have been replaced by shopping centres. Two things that Maclean would definitely have approved of, however, are that there are far fewer public houses in the Shaws than a century ago – and far fewer churches as well. Or rather three things. In lieu of death duties, the daughter of Sir John Maxwell left Pollok estate to the city of Glasgow, and it is now a public park, not a private estate, which has twice won the Best Park in Europe award. Maclean would have seen that as progress.

But the last ten years have not been altogether happy times for the Shaws. Although four of the high-rise blocks in Shawhill Road have been renovated, many of the other multis have been demolished and so far only very partially replaced by new social and private housing. The baths and sports centre has been closed and demolished, and the John Maxwell School has also been closed due to falling population and is decaying rapidly, giving the whole central area of the Shaws a desolate look. This is not mitigated by the local 1960s shopping centre, which looks as if it had been built as an SAS counter-insurgency training centre. Only the Burgh Hall and the library remains, and the latter is a much more welcoming building inside than its outward appearance indicates, and worth a visit.

Bounded by the River Cart, a dual carriageway and the railway line, the Pollokshaws Triangle is still very much a village, with a community feel to it. Most people know most people, and talking to them you discover that they still know of John Maclean. A century after the outbreak of the Imperialist War, which launched the 20th century on its tragic trajectory, and which Maclean so steadfastly opposed, let us also not forget him or his example.

CHAPTER TWO

Govanhill Retro

IF YOU WISHED to make a film depicting working-class life in Glasgow before 1914, there would be no need to establish a film set. All you would have to do would be to set it in Govanhill. No other area in the city retains so many of its Victorian and Edwardian tenements, as well as the intact street grid plan along which they were laid out. Further, Govanhill holds onto, in one form or another, almost all its built civic amenities: public park, hospital, library, burgh hall, volunteer drill halls, churches, public baths and steamie – from a century ago. Govanhill remains an unrivalled cameo of pre-1914 working-class Glasgow.

I lived off Govanhill's Victoria Road for a couple of years when I came to Glasgow four decades ago. One of my habitations was in Langside Road in a good working-class tenement with living room, bedroom, kitchen and bathroom – and a tiled wally close. Though I had a bath, I had no washing machine, so I used the steamie as well as the swimming baths, read the papers in the local library and strolled in Queen's Park on fine days. There was a huge variety of shops on Allison Street: many, like the watchmakers, the delicatessen and shoe-makers, were still owned by Jews, and one could hear Yiddish spoken on entering. There were plenty of decent pubs, and Neeson's used to deliver up the finest pint of Guinness then obtainable outside Ireland, once you waded through the cigarette ends to the bar, and through the even deeper brogue of Irish regulars who had come across to Glasgow in the boom years of the 1950s and '60s to work. Separated from the Gorbals (then at its lowest ebb) by only a railway line, Govanhill was an entirely different working-class world. Govanhill was an area people wanted to live in, and was one of the few inner-city work-ing-class districts of Glasgow that had not lost population in the pre-vious decades. Govanhill was helped by the fact that its industry lay outside its residential areas, yet was readily accessible to the popula-tion. There was very little hereabouts until the early 19th century, when the lands of Govanhill began to be dotted with miners' rows. Many of the mines were opened after 1822 by William Dixon, the first of a dynasty of English coal and ironmasters who moved to Glasgow.

Dixon built his own primitive railway, with horse-drawn wagons, to carry his coal to the river. Using this coal, the second William Dixon opened the Govan Iron Works in 1839, on lands between Govanhill and the Gorbals. By 1842, when the factory inspector paid him a visit and left a report, Dixon employed 800 workers at this works and was one of the biggest coal and iron capitalists in the west of Scotland. The inspector also recorded Dixon's iron grip on his men, who worked a ten-hour day – or more. No membership of any unions or other organisations was allowed, and child labour was widespread. Dixon did, however, provide rudimentary schooling, a library and other cultural activities for his workers. He was an argumentative and litigious man and spent a staggering £250,000 on lawsuits, many unsuccessful, which brought the company into financial difficulties.

William 'Crimea' Simpson painted a fine watercolour of the works in the 1840s; its blast furnaces viewed from Govanhill, then still largely open spaces. Dixon's iron works became known as 'Dixon's Blazes,' a commentator observing that 'the bright glare cheers a long winter's night'. But the Govanhill coal mines were soon worked out and the third William Dixon feued the land thereabouts out for housing from 1869. This led to the construction, between then and 1900, of Govanhill as it largely remains today. By 1900 the last of the old miners' 'raws' had also been demolished. The first church built in Govanhill, interestingly enough, was a Wesleyan Methodist one, probably built for the large number of English ironworkers Dixon brought from Shropshire to work at the Govan Iron Works. Govanhill became a burgh in 1877 and Dixon the Third donated Dixon Hall as its offices. But he also donated the same building to Crosshill, a middle-class development actually in Renfrewshire, which achieved burgh status at the same time (Govanhill was in Lanarkshire). The municipal building was divided internally, and had two entrances, one for each burgh.

The Govanhill Library came along in 1906, one of those designed by J Rhind following the Carnegie bequest to the city, and the steamie and public baths followed before 1914. The Samaritan Hospital built 'for the care of poor women' was opened in 1903, an interesting building with lots of Art Nouveau and Arts and Crafts details in its construction. It is now flatted accommodation. Govanhill had its own park, a small area bought by the council to prevent over-building, but Queen's Park, one of the city's finest, lay to the south. This was laid out by James Paxton, who designed the Crystal Palace Exhibition in London. In Queen's Park many years ago I had one of those experiences hard to have outside Glasgow. I was sitting sunning

Govanhill

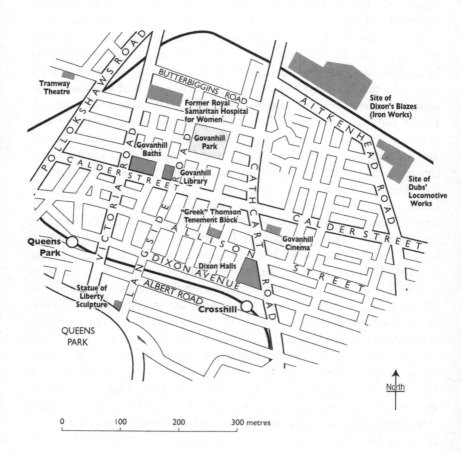

Govanhill Route Summary

1   Take a train to Crosshill station.

2   Walk down Cathcart Road to Calder Street (Govanhill cinema is on the right).

3   Walk along to Aitkenhead Road and continue southbound to Butterbiggins Road (taking a possible diversion to The Tramway).

4   Go back up Victoria Road, turn left into Calder Street with Govanhill Baths and the library first and second on the left.

5   Go down Langside Road to Allison Street.

6   Take a left, eastbound turn to the Greek Thomson tenement

7   Go back by Dixon Halls to Crosshill station.

Approximate route time: 2.5 hours

myself on a bench when a Glesca character, the waur for drink, came and sat beside the two Norwegian girls on the next bench. Sensing their anxiety I decided to keep a Galahadish eye on the situation.

After a suitable pause he asked where they were from, and was told Norway, and that they were holidaying in Scotland.

'Name five famous Scotsmen,' he demanded of them.

Before they could reply he rattled off a dozen or so, to the surprise of the girls, but not to me. I'd seen this Glesca floorshow before. But not the next bit, I hadn't.

'Name five famous Norwegians,' he further demanded. Astonishment rather than ignorance probably prevented the girls replying, before he said: 'Ibsen, Grieg – bit his ancestors were Scottish – Amundsen, Munch... and Quisling, but he was a bastard and hardly coonts.'

Having achieved his desired effect, he rose and walked off. You get a better class of underclass in Glasgow.

Another example of Glasgow gallusness can be seen on the splendid 'tenement' – though that is hardly an appropriate word for a building as fine as this – which graces the corner of Langside Road and Queen's Drive facing the park. Look up and on the highest corner, the year after its prototype was raised in New York, stands a full life-sized sandstone replica of the Statue of Liberty.

In 1868, Queen's Park FC played their first game in Queen's Park and the Govanhill folk soon had both Hampden and Cathkin, home of Third Lanark, on their doorsteps. It is worth mentioning here that a Queen's Park player, Andrew Watson, was the first black footballer in the UK, and when capped for Scotland in 1881 was the first ever black football internationalist, and he played in a 6–1 victory over England.

The 1920s cinema boom created no less than four cinemas in Govanhill, all of which eventually closed and were demolished apart from the Govanhill Cinema in Bank Hall Street, built in 1925. Though its interior was gutted, the tiled exterior remains, an eclectic mix of a Moorish mosque and a Hindu temple, and is appropriate to the fantasy world created by the early cinema.

Further to all these delights, the good folk of Govanhill also had their own local dancehall, the Plaza at Eglinton Toll. This was for some time the only venue in once-dance-crazy Glasgow to escape closure, but has sadly now also closed its doors. But it was not so much the extensive provision of social facilities that marked Govanhill out at this time; rather it was the quality of the housing.

The houses constructed in Govanhill were amongst the best for

working people, not only in Glasgow but also possibly in Britain, at this time. Virtually all the tenement houses built had internal sanitation, very unusual then. They were also constructed to a minimum specification of two rooms, lowering the population density. The high quality of the Govanhill tenements is emphasised by the fact that in 1875, no less an architect than Alexander 'Greek' Thomson built a block of them in Allison Street. In 1891 when it was annexed by Glasgow, Govanhill had a population of about 15,000; the adjacent Gorbals covered almost exactly the same surface area, and had a population of 50,000. The district managed to maintain this enviable status: in

Govanhill Cinema:
Govanhill was well-supplied with a variety of amenities, including several cinemas, of which this Hindu/Moslem dream palace off Aitkenhead Road survives, though it is no longer in use as a cinema.

a survey of the city in 1935, less than three per cent of the population was living in single ends in Govanhill, the sixth lowest rate for any city ward – including the middle-class areas. In the period of comprehensive development in the 1960s and '70s, parts of eastern Govanhill were demolished and replaced by new housing. But the local people fought against wholesale demolition, and formed housing associations to work for the restoration of Govanhill, rather than its destruction. Later, in the 1990s, they waged a bitter and initially unsuccessful campaign against the closure of Govanhill baths, as the council sought to centralise such facilities in newer sports complexes. Later, to their credit, Glasgow Council partly retreated and has given support to a local trust, which is in the process of reopening the baths as both a sports and a cultural focus for the community.

Just along from the baths in Calder Street stands Rhind's splendid library from 1906, where Govanhill's most famous son spent much of his early years: there is a photograph of him on the wall inside. RD Laing was to become famous (or infamous) in the 1960s with his views on schizophrenia, expressed in works such as *Sanity, Madness and the Family*, and his unorthodox opinions about drug usage, including LSD, in therapy. He was born in a tenement just behind the Govanhill Library, at 21 Ardbeg Street where there is currently a commemorative plaque. His views on madness as being caused by social tensions within the family have some support from his own experience.

His parents were aspirant working class, the mother's ideas of respectability including the denial of ever having had sex, even after giving birth, and the father was a skilled electrical engineer with the mining equipment firm of Mavour and Coulson and then Glasgow Corporation, with social ambitions for his family and his son, for whom he managed to get a scholarship to the fee-paying Hutchesons School, then located in the Gorbals. Laing 'crossed the tracks' to Glasgow University and then moved to an elite psychiatric practice in London, retaining no fond memories of Govanhill or indeed of Glasgow. 'The quickest way out of Glasgow is several stiff whiskies,' he was reputed to have said, and he was troubled by drug and alcohol problems throughout life.

Railways often form social and territorial borders, and this is clear if you get off the train at Crosshill station. Crosshill was built as a middle-class suburb of Glasgow from the 1860s, and its grand villas and, later, terraces facing Queens Park were originally far from, but eventually approached by, Govanhill. Crosshill had a population of

4,000 when it was incorporated into Glasgow in 1891, dwarfed by its working-class neighbour, which you enter as soon as you drop down the hill from the station. Dixon Halls is directly in front of you, an attractive if architecturally undistinguished building now serving as a day centre. East along Allison Street takes you to Aitkenhead Road, and Polmadie.

If Crosshill was Govanhill's posh satellite, then Polmadie was its underbelly, though not without its civic pride, according to the refrain:

> Napoleon was the Emperor
> And he ruled the land and sea
> He was king o France and Germany
> But he never ruled Polmadie

Between Cathcart Road and Aitkenhead Road the housing is not always of the standard achieved further west and hereabouts is where some tenement demolition took place. This was the possibly less desirable end of Govanhill, as it lay next to the industrial district. Dixon's Blazes was just across the railway line at this point, with its noise and pollution, and the Caledonian Railway repair workshops were also set up here in 1879. On the Govanhill side of the railway too were several industrial units of interest. One was 'the yard where many boats were built but never one launched'. The Sentinel Works was opened in 1880. Here on Polmadie Road and Jessie Street, 1,000 men prefabricated small river and lake craft which were exported and then assembled at their destinations, the lakes of Africa and Asia, and the rivers of South America. Apparently, never a boat showed a fault when reassembled on the other side of the globe, a testimony to the skills of the workforce. Today the factory serves as a poverty-stop car boot sales location and the area around resembles some post-apocalyptic nightmare. If you like that sort of thing, it's the place for you on a rainy Saturday.

But the most important works in Polmadie were the Queen's Park Locomotive Works, established in 1864 by the German engineer and entrepreneur Henry Dubs. Many of Glasgow's entrepreneurs came from Fürth, the German city, but a few also came from Darmstadt, where Dubs had been born. Dubs had worked in the Springburn locomotive industry, but broke out on his own. He was very successful and soon employed 2,500 men. Dubs was also the first major engineering works in Glasgow to employ women in the drawing office. By his death in 1876 he had made a fortune of £120,000, (multiplying

by a factor of 100 produces today's equivalent value for this sum) and
the works were producing 100 locomotives a year. Fierce competition
caused Queen's Park to amalgamate with the North British Locomotive Company in 1905, and the works shared the fate of their parent
when they closed in 1962 – just two years short of their centenary.
Though it had a different pronunciation, Dubs' name was spelt the
same as the old Scotch word for mud, and the works were known as
The Dubs. That his workers may have had other problems than mud
is shown by the following refrain:

> We're railwaymen at Polmadie
> In a hotter place you couldn'a be
> And when in Hell we gaither when we dee
> We'll be nane the waur than in Polmadie.

Just before the closure of the Queen's Park Locomotive Works, the
Govan Iron Works had also shut their doors in 1959, as did most of
the other industrial units in Polmadie. Today there are some ware-
housing facilities in the former locomotive works, and the nearby
council's rubbish incinerator, whose huge towers dominated the
skyline, has recently been demolished as well. Post-industrial
Polmadie has replaced its industrial forebear. From Aitkenhead Road,
we cross Cathcart Road again and find the delightfully named Butterbiggins Road.

That Govanhill had a pre-industrial history is shown by the name
of this street, which divides a bus depot from the Royal Samaritan
Hospital, now converted into housing. The name Butterbiggins Road
refers to a time when there was a dairy here, and the local population
still spoke broad Scots, for biggins is the word for buildings. This
street carries you onto the main thoroughfare of Govanhill, Victoria
Road. This is a fine street of well-maintained sandstone tenements
and mainly good quality shops, ending in the heights of Queen's Park.

On Coplaw Street, across Victoria Road, there used to be a Jewish
theatre where the Avron Greenbaum Players put on regular and excellent dramatic performances. I attended a couple of these when I lived
in Govanhill, and the audience was predominantly Jewish. Like the
newspaper the *Jewish Echo*, which used to be located a little north of
here at St Andrew's Cross, this theatre has sadly gone, and a block of
flats has taken the place of the building which housed it. But Govanhill
still has a theatrical life. At the end of Coplaw Street where it joins
Pollokshaws Road, was located the old Corporation Tramway Works,

where Glasgow's wonderful trams were constructed from 1899 onwards. This building later became the Transport Museum, and latterly has become, in the Tramway Theatre, one of the most interesting locations for theatrical productions in Scotland, as well as art exhibitions and other cultural events. Out back is the wonderful Hidden Garden, a green oasis of tranquility in the busy city.

A stroll down Victoria Road leads to Allison Street. Allison Street is more *vif* and demotic than Victoria Road, and where once were Jewish shopkeepers, the shops and the neighbouring tenements are now increasingly being occupied by Glasgow's immigrant Muslim community. The Pakistanis have been a great boon to Glasgow, making it not only the curry capital of the UK, but also bringing in some welcome additions to the local genetic stock in the form of the gallus lads and gorgeous lassies of their community. Where Allison Street joins Cathcart Road, you are back at the Dixon Halls, and Crosshill station.

When I first wrote this chapter a decade ago, I concluded with the words, 'Going back, Govanhill still seems to be a comfortable place to live'. In many ways this remains true, but it would be willful to ignore the social issues that have emerged in the district in a fairly brief period of time. In the last decade there has been a new immigration into certain areas of Govanhill, largely from Eastern Europe and further afield. This has led to the creation of ghettoes where gang masters and slum landlords have fostered problems of overcrowding and decay in the physical fabric of many tenement blocks, with a negative impact on the wider community of the area. Ignoring these issues simply leaves the door open for the activities of racialists, and is not an option.

The City Council identified a group of tenement blocks in southeast Govanhill, and with the help of funding from the Scottish Government, has stated its resolution of acquiring them by compulsory purchase for transformation into housing association properties. This should help in preventing an area, long known for the high quality of its working-class housing, becoming instead one blighted with enclaves reproducing the worst squalor of the past.

For information on, or to help with, Govanhill Baths Community Trust, see www.govanhillbaths.com or 0141 433 2999 (not Monday).

CHAPTER THREE

Gorbals: A New Glasgow Suburb

IN THE EARLY YEARS of the 19th century, the burghers of Glasgow looked across the river and saw, adjacent to the existing village of Gorbals, a prestigious example of Regency town planning rising on the southern bank of the Clyde. The aristocratic names of its streets reflected its aspirations: Bedford, Eglinton, and Norfolk. After two checkered centuries, half-way through which the Gorbals became identified as one of Europe's worst slums, the wheel is turning if not fully, at least part circle, and the area is again being developed as a desirable place to live. The Gorbals of *No Mean City* and the gangster world of Jimmy Boyle is fast disappearing, if not already gone. The Gorbals today is the site of what must be one of the most successful regeneration schemes undertaken anywhere.

Emerging into daylight at Bridge Street subway station, such an urban renaissance is not immediately apparent. Around you are large tracts of derelict land, functioning mainly as commuter car parks, but Bridge Street contains some fine buildings, albeit in sad states of disrepair. These include James Millar's impressive Bridge Street station, designed for the Caledonian Railway and a fine Glasgow Savings Bank on the opposite, eastern side. But 75 years before these were built, this area was the site of the development of Laurieston, Glasgow's newest suburb, which the Laurie brothers hoped would make their fortune. Carlton Place, fronting the Clyde, was the jewel in the crown of this development and thankfully is fully extant today, though functioning as offices and not as the original housing. Laurieston House here was deemed grand enough to host George IV on his projected Glasgow trip of 1822 – only he never visited the city to see the interiors that had been done by the same Italian artists who decorated his own Windsor Castle. Though much of Laurieston was never built due to the bankruptcy of the Lauries, it is a mistake to see the Gorbals area as falling immediately into universal decay.

Much quality middle-class housing continued to be erected after the Lauries' plans were abandoned, such as Abbotsford Place in the

Gorbals

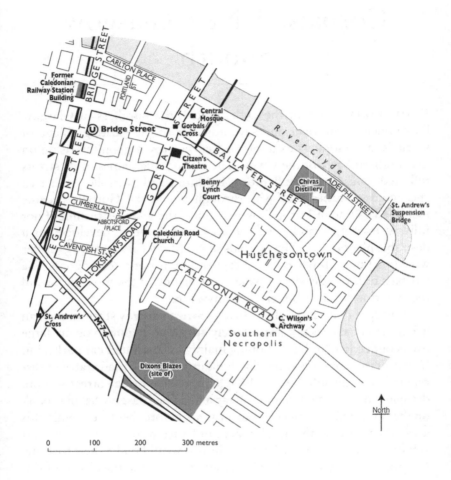

Gorbals Route Summary

1   Take the subway to Bridge Street.

2   Go down Bridge Street and onto Carlton Place.

3   Make your way to Gorbals Cross (Citizens Theatre) and then along Ballater Street, with a possible diversion onto the St Andrew's suspension bridge and the Clyde Waterfront.

4   Explore your way through Hutchesontown to arrive at Caledonia Road (Southern Necropolis).

5   Head west to the Caledonia Road church and view the staggering modern flats there.

6   Continue down Pollokshaws Road to St Andrew's Cross and then back up Eglinton Street to Bridge Street subway.

Approximate route time: 2.5 hours

1830s. Each dwelling here had seven or eight rooms, with a mews for the horse-carriage out back. Examination of the mid-19th century censuses shows that Laurieston retained its middle-class status until well after many think, and it was only the development of the suburban railways, connected to new housing around the Queen's Park area to the south, which caused the middle classes to finally leave the area. In 1872, Tweed's *Guide to Glasgow and the Clyde* described a walk down Eglinton Street and noted the many 'graceful buildings' in this 'fine street', recommending to the tourist a circular walk through the area – which he would hardly have done were it a slum. Even in the 1930s, Abbotsford Place was known as the Harley Street of Glasgow, and seeing photographs of the wonderful, now-demolished buildings, would make you weep for their loss – a wholly preventable one.

Heading south down Eglinton Street today is sadly not the experience it was in Tweed's time, and virtually nothing remains from that period – indeed from any but the most recent era. Passing a 1930s cinema (restored initially as the highly successful Carling Academy, now the O2, a rock concert venue) leads you towards a landscape of derelict railway viaducts, waste ground and some examples of 1970s housing at its least imaginative. At the corner of Cavendish Street is a 1980s red-brick dwelling, admittedly better than its '70s neighbours, but a mere shadow of what it replaced. Here till 1980 stood

one of the glories of Alexander 'Greek' Thomson, his Queen's Park
Terrace block of middle-class tenements, constructed between 1856
and 1860. Though subsequently suffering multiple occupancy and
deterioration, their demolition by Glasgow District Council was one
of the greatest acts of vandalism in the city's history. Thomson, probably Glasgow and Scotland's most original 19th-century architect,
lived in this desirable area himself, at Apsley Street from 1847–57,
when he designed Queen's Park Terrace.

Passing under the recently constructed extension to the M74 motorway, and a little to the south Cavendish Street, where Eglinton Street
– and the Gorbals – ends at St Andrews Cross, lies a row of rather
scruffy shops. Here, until 1992, one of the premises housed the offices
of the *Jewish Echo*, Glasgow's own English-language weekly Jewish
newspaper, published since 1928, when it replaced earlier Yiddish
publications. As the Glasgow middle classes left Laurieston, their
houses became sub-let and were occupied by new arrivals, amongst
whom the Jews from Eastern Europe were to be the most prominent.
By 1885, half of the children at the nearby Abbotsford Primary School
were Jewish. The community – about 10,000 souls – was large enough
to support the building of a synagogue in South Portland Street, the
establishment of a Talmud Torah school and a Zionist reading room.
But organisations that integrated the Jews into Glasgow life were also
founded, such as the Oxford Star football team, and the Jewish Lads
Brigade, which boasted the only all-Jewish pipe band in the world.
Green's Kosher Hotel in Abbotsford Place was a point of arrival or
transit for many Jews fleeing persecution first from Czarist Russia and
then from Nazi Germany. Glasgow Council organised meetings in
1892 to protest against persecution of the Jews in Russia, and in 1933
boycotted German goods in protest against Hitler's anti-Semitism.
Many of the Jews worked in the sweated trades and were active in
the early trade union and socialist movements, like 'Manny' Shinwell,
Glasgow's adoptive Jew and Red Clydesider. Others, like Isaac Woolf-
son, made their mark on the business world – or in the arts, such as the
sculptor Benno Schotz. And in Meyer Galpern, Glasgow Provost in the
1950s, Glasgow had the UK's first ever Jewish civic leader.

A fascinating picture of Jewish life in the Gorbals is given in
Ralph Glasser's *Growing Up in the Gorbals* (1986). The son of a
Jewish immigrant, Glasser worked in the textile trade before winning
a scholarship to Oxford. His book describes the Gorbals of the '30s
with its gangs, appalling housing conditions and unemployment.

Glaser recalls coming out of school and seeing workless men waiting in hope outside Dixon's ironworks:

> Outside the twenty foot high gates were clustered a couple of dozen men in cloth caps, fustian jackets and mufflers, heavy black trousers tied with string below the knees. Lantern jawed, faces glazed with cold, collars turned up under their ears and heads bowed, they stood huddled upon themselves, sheltering as sheep do on a storm-swept hillside. These men waited on a stroke of luck, a call for extra hands.

He also contrasts the older Jewish political world with its philosophical Kropotkinite anarchism centred round the cosy stove and library of the Workers' Circle, with the attractions of communism to himself and the younger Jews of the period, faced with the war in Spain and Nazi anti-Semitism.

The Gorbals' reputation as a centre of political radicalism goes back earlier than the 1930s, however. John Maclean's connections with the Gorbals are many. As early as January 1918 he was appointed by the new Bolshevik Government in Russia as their Consul in Scotland. At 12 Portland Street, just behind Carlton Place, Maclean set up his office. His mail was censored, his Russian secretary arrested and deported, and money sent to him was blocked. Maclean sent out an appeal for financial help to labour organisations and for 'all class-conscious international workers to stand by our Russian comrades'. His work included helping political refugees get back to Russia after the Revolution of 1917. He also organised help for the dependents of the Russian and Lithuanian coal miners in Lanarkshire. These men, not British citizens, had been forcibly enlisted in the Russian army by Britain in 1917 and their families were destitute.

In the period after the First World War, John Maclean's work had an especial focus on the Gorbals, where he stood twice for parliament. In 1918 he was endorsed by the anti-war Gorbals Labour Party – the British Socialist Party to which Maclean now belonged had re-affiliated to Labour. He stood against a pro-war candidate supported and enforced by the Labour Party nationally; Maclean got 7,500 votes against 14,000 for the pro-war Barnes. He stood again as an independent communist in 1922, campaigning for a Scottish Workers' Republic, and by this time he was being aided in his Gorbals and other work by Harry McShane. Though defeated, he polled a respectable number of votes – over 4,000 in 1922 against the ILP candidate.

But this was the period of Maclean's political decline, when he made a series of disastrous errors. Firstly he stood aloof from the newly formed Communist Party, and secondly he emphasised more and more Scottish independence, misinspired by events in Ireland. Maclean's integrity can never be faulted, but in the years after 1919 his political judgement increasingly has to be. For example, he was convinced that Britain would soon go to war with the USA, and such a conviction informed many of his political actions. Though still personally revered, he was increasingly politically isolated, and even his loyal lieutenant Harry McShane abandoned Maclean for the Communist Party.

In his autobiography, *No Mean Fighter* (1978), McShane observes:

> We had conducted the best propaganda and agitation in the
> West of Scotland, but we had left no organisation behind us.
> I knew I had to join an organisation. I joined the Communist
> Party in 1922. This meant a complete break with John Maclean.

The next year, McShane was being evicted from his house in the Gorbals and a large crowd gathered to contest the eviction. Another crowd came to give their support, led by Maclean, but they didn't speak. Poignantly, McShane states, 'We looked at each other, saw each other, and I never saw him again'.

But back to our urban ramble. At St Andrews Cross, I once entered the Star Bar for a sustaining and cheap plate of mince and tatties. Whilst waiting with my half-pint I asked the barmaid if we were in the Gorbals, and she emphatically answered, 'Yes'. The other pub inmates joined in and to a man – no women there – agreed that this was the case, indeed seemed slightly chagrined that there might be any doubt in the matter. 'What's up there?' I asked, pointing southwards to the other side of the Cross, a mere 20 yards away. There were a variety of replies, much self-confessed ignorance, and, basically, an almost complete lack of interest.

At the gushet of St Andrews Cross, Pollokshaws Road leads back north towards the Gorbals, passing the fine old Abbotsford School (after it closed as a school it became a business centre, but that too has closed and at present the building lies unused) on our left, set amidst piecemeal housing development and land that has lain dere-lict for over 30 years. Arriving at Gorbals Street, we enter territory with a much more ancient pedigree than Laurieston, which we have just walked through. The Gorbals has medieval origins and was at one time Glasgow's leper colony. It grew to a population of 5,000 by 1800, and had swelled to 36,000 by the time it was annexed by Glasgow in 1846. At this time Gorbals Cross was still a cluster of buildings, many dating from the 17th century. But the old baronial dwellings had been subdivided into festering slums and the back lands were breeding grounds of squalor. This situation worsened when the Gorbals became one of the favoured settlement areas for the impoverished Irish immigrants who poured into Scotland from the 1840s. One observer commented in the 1850s:

> We are really grieved to part with some of these old landmarks of the city, and we cannot help urging the proprietors of such houses as exist to pay some little attention to them, and above all to prevent them falling prey to the hordes of Irish immigrants who have a fancy to burrow in these ancient spots.

But those that did not fall into ruin were swept away by the City Improvement Trust from the 1870s, and by 1900 the area around Gorbals Street was entirely tenemented. The amazing thing is that this Gorbals, too, has almost totally vanished in its turn (as too has the high-rise world that replaced the tenements in the 1960s). On Gorbals Street remains one empty and derelict tenement, James Salmon II's fine British Linen Bank building, and nothing else, except at its southern end a pub, the stump of a former tenement, which brazenly states its allegiance to Celtic FC (unsurprising given the fact that Celtic greats

Oxford Star Jewish football team circa 1910: Glasgow had a Jewish pipe band, as well as sporting organisations such as Oxford Star. These helped break down social barriers and later enabled the city to have the first Jewish civic leader in the UK.

Pat Crerand and Charlie Gallacher hailed from the Gorbals, though its most famous sporting son was the boxer Benny Lynch, now commemorated in Benny Lynch Court in Hutchesontown). Here, too, is found the Citizens Theatre, which has had its exterior (in the form of a set of statues) moved inside for safe keeping. The 'Citz' was originally the Princess' Theatre, more in the music hall tradition, till it was taken over by James Bridie, the playwright, in 1945. Under the now-departed Giles Havergal, it became one of Europe's most renowned theatre companies.

To the north of the Citz, across what once was Gorbals Cross and is now a windy, littered set of traffic lights, lies the Glasgow Central Mosque. Though you will see few Asian faces in the Gorbals today, it was initially the main area of Asian settlement in Scotland, with up to 10,000 living there, and it even boasted a newspaper, *The Young Muslim*. When the tenements were demolished the Asians had little claim on, or desire to live in, the new council housing, and, like the Jews before them, moved out. Nevertheless, the new mosque was built here and opened in 1984. One inadvertent side effect of redevelopment in the Gorbals has been to turn what was once Glasgow's most multi-racial inner-city area into what is now probably its least.

From the former Gorbals Cross, Ballater Street leads eastwards into Hutchesontown. Although this too was begun as a prestige development, it appears to have gone downmarket long before Laurieston, despite its facing Glasgow Green. Possibly the opening of Dixon's Blazes iron works in 1839 on the southern edge of Hutchesontown, on the site of Dixon's existing coal mines, had something to do with this. We should remember, however, that the Victorians didn't have our anti-industrial bias, and indeed Dixon's Blazes was something of a tourist attraction. Tweed comments in his *Guide to Glasgow and the Clyde* (1872) that:

> The stranger who wishes to see in full operation one of the most extensive and important of local industries should spend an hour or two in visiting the works, admission to which will readily be granted on application.

Certainly, Hutchesontown became much more industrialised than Laurieston, with low-paid unskilled and semi-skilled work predominating. (Dixon's higher-paid workers lived in Govanhill, an area of better-quality working-class housing to the south of the Blazes.) By 1900 this poverty, allied to overcrowding, which was phenomenal even by Glasgow standards, meant that the area had infant mortality and premature death rates many times the city average. Even in 1951, the Gorbals had a population of 50,000 crowded into what one writer described as the area of an average-sized dairy farm.

The Hutchesontown area was carpet-bombed by the developments in the 1960s and '70s, and there was hardly a single historical building left standing. In Ballater Street there remains but one lone tenement, dating from 1903, displaying the Co-operative handshake emblem. Just north by the river is what must be the last manufacturing unit left in the Gorbals, a distillery currently operated by Chivas. Little more than the odd public building – such as the public library and the predominantly Catholic churches (for this was the heart of Glasgow's Irish community) – remained amidst the tower blocks erected at that time. The old tenements were replaced by experiments in social engineering, which were of limited success. The notorious 'Hutchie E' maze of precast concrete wind tunnels was rendered rubble as early as 1987, while the knighthood-winning Basil Spence's Queen Elizabeth Court tower blocks followed them to dust in 1993. In consequence, the population of the Gorbals had been reduced to 10,000 by 2001 – 20 per cent of what it had been half a century before. It is Hutchesontown that is undergoing the most intensive redevelopment of mixed housing association and private housing, and walking around the area is an uplifting experience, showing off the advantages of coherent and human-scale town planning. There is even a new hotel in the area, taking advantage of the Gorbals' proximity to the town centre.

It is worth taking a side trail off Ballater Street to Adelphi Street and the St Andrews Suspension Bridge over the Clyde; amongst the tree-lined river banks one could almost imagine oneself by the Seine. Crossing Ballater Street again into McNeil Street there is found a mix of renovated and newly built housing, with imaginative street furniture. Here, too, is another of Rhind's magnificent libraries, probably the finest of them all, but sadly no longer operating as a centre of local learning. The remaining high-rise blocks here (not everyone hated the high life) are being reclad to soften their look and blend with the new buildings. You can wander for ages around Hutchesontown with profit, but eventually you should emerge onto Caledonia Road, beside the Southern Necropolis, which thankfully appears to be getting better maintenance than formerly. Here in lair 3971 lies the vault of Thomas Lipton, the Gorbals boy, born of poor Irish (though Protestant) immigrant parents, who became a millionaire by the time he was 30 with his chain of grocery shops. Also buried here is Alexander 'Greek' Thomson, and a further point of interest is the (alas, dilapidated) gatehouse, designed by Charles Wilson.

On the north side of Caledonia Road are found some of the larger new houses, built in a stunning style, that gives the lie to those who think modern architecture is worthless; these buildings would grace any European city. Across from them, next to the Necropolis, is the site of Dixon's Blazes, closed in 1962, now a rather unlovely trading estate. But just adjacent, like something out of Athens or Rome, stands the shell of Alexander Thomson's Caledonia Road Church (the tenements he built flanking it are long gone). When this church lost its congregation, Glasgow Council bought it with a view to restoration. This never took place, and instead the building became a target for vandals – now all that remains are the walls and spire. So little survives in the Gorbals of the historical environment that the salvation of this church must be a priority: indeed, given Thomson's status, it must be a national and international priority. This will give Glasgow Council the chance to atone for its other Thomson sins, and the church could be the focal point of the new Gorbals itself, as regeneration spreads westwards from Hutchesontown towards central Gorbals and Laurieston.

Walking along Cumberland Street are the early signs of this, with new medium-slung flatted buildings following the line of the street, being constructed in the place of the demolished or to be demolished tower blocks. In Gorbals Street, too, the street-line is being restored. The abolition of the street was probably the greatest crime of '60s and '70s redevelopment: its rediscovery a main virtue of new architecture. At the end of Cumberland Street we are back on Eglinton Street, and once again near Bridge Street subway – or one can walk a little further to Carlton Place and view Laurieston House. Crossing the river by the suspension bridge reminds you that, however hard life was in the Gorbals, it was always only ten minutes from the city centre and ten minutes from the Green. And maybe this time, after Regency suburb, Victorian tenement slum and concrete jungle, the planners have got it right in the Gorbals, and would appear to have achieved regeneration without gentrification and social cleansing.

CHAPTER FOUR

The Glories of Govan

READERS NOTING THE title of this section might think that I could only be referring to the footballing exploits of Rangers FC – familiar as they might be with the picture of Govan drawn by the string-vested philosopher Rab C Nesbitt as a place not of glory, but of inner-city decay and drunks in Wine Alley. Rest assured, readers, that as an Aberdeen supporter, Govan's glories for me have nothing to do with Ibrox Stadium, magnificent though its architecturally A-listed South Stand might be, and that, though Rab does describe with humour an aspect of Govan life that is really no laughing matter, there is far more to Govan than is shown in his philosophy. It has to be admitted here, nevertheless, that Ibrox (and Parkhead) saw some of the best afternoons of my life. In the 1970s and 1980s, with great regularity, Aberdeen FC would come to Glasgow and hammer the Old Firm. The greatest moment was when my old primary school football teammate, Jocky Scott, scored three in a 5–1 gubbing of the 'Gers. But those days, like Govan's industry, will probably not return.

Where to begin, and convince you quickly of my argument? Nowhere better than by jumping on Glasgow's Clockwork Orange subway at any point and emerging – where sadly few but locals do – at Cessnock station. Immediately on exiting you notice the unusual ironwork and motifs of the station's entry arch; look at the tenement above the station, in whose bowels on Walmer Crescent the subway was tunneled, and you will see that the station arch is echoing the motifs round the doorways of the building. The subway was built in the 1890s linking Govan with the West End of Glasgow, and when it was renovated in the 1980s the ironwork was added as a way of paying tribute to the genius of the architect of Walmer Crescent, which was built by Alexander 'Greek' Thomson in 1857. Though it is on the official Thomson Heritage Trail, few people come to see it as they do his city centre and suburban buildings, because of its location – and, sadly, condition. The Crescent consists of a mix of flyblown hotels and multiple occupancies – with some vacant and occasionally burned out, combined with brave attempts to restore and regenerate other parts of this fine row.

Govan

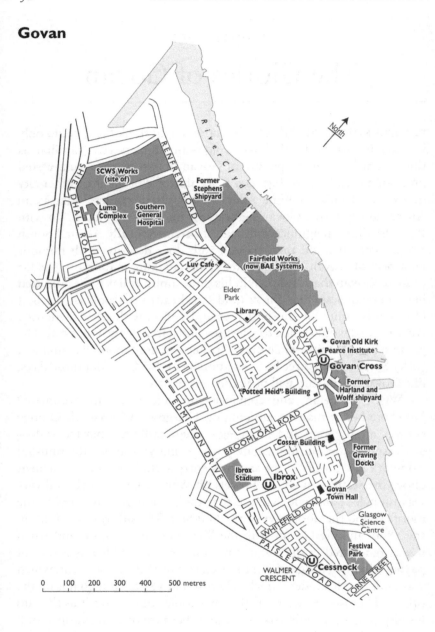

Govan Route Summaries

Route 1

1 Take the subway to Cessnock and Walmer Crescent.

2 Head east to Lorne Street then north past Festival Park to the Glasgow Science Centre.

3 Proceed westwards to the former Govan Town Hall on Govan Road and continue along this street until you reach Govan Cross. (Pearce Institute, Govan Old Kirk.)

4 After possibly enjoying a refreshment in The Pearce Institute, double back to the 'Potted Heid' building.

5 Head southwards down Broomloan Road to Ibrox Stadium, from whence Edmiston Drive and the PR (Paisley Road) take you back to Cessnock Subway.

Approximate route time: 2.5 hours

Route 2

1 Take the subway to Govan Cross and investigate all its treasures.

2 Head west along the Govan Road, past the Fairfield Shipbuilding and Engineering Company building on the right, observing its grand office doorway and sculptures, until you reach Linthouse at Renfrew Road (possible refreshments at the LUV café).

3 Continue past the old Southern General Hospital, then past the former site of the Co-op at Shieldhall, until you reach Shieldhall Road and the Luma Tower.

4 Negotiate the underpass at Shieldhall Road and get onto Langlands Road, which will take you to the Elder Park (Elder Park Library and several fine sculptures).

5 Head back to Govan Cross and the subway there.

Approximate route time: 3 hours

A previous stone clean was badly done and did more harm than good, and the ironwork is in similar condition to the stonework. Yet a dentist's surgery allowed me entry to see Thomson's interior plaster-work, stenciling and woodwork. These features are on a modest scale compared to some of his buildings, for this was a crescent (i.e. flats) not a terrace (i.e. a storeyed house). Originally standing alone in open countryside, it housed respectable families of professionals and small businessmen, before it declined to slum status in the 1920s as Govan's middle class fled to the suburbs. Set back from Paisley Road, the Cres-cent is fronted by a promenade of shops (formerly this was the small private garden of the Crescent) now sadly also in disrepair and reflect-ing, in the wares on sale, the poverty of the local inhabitants. Unless something is done soon, this building will go the way of Thomson's other wonderful tenement, the Gorbals' Queen's Park Terrace, which was demolished in the 1980s. Visit Walmer Crescent, publicise its plight: save it.

East from Walmer Crescent, Paisley Road West – 'the PR' as it is locally known – leads you to Lorne Street, which flanks the Festival Park, a legacy of the Garden Festival of 1988 and a welcome addition

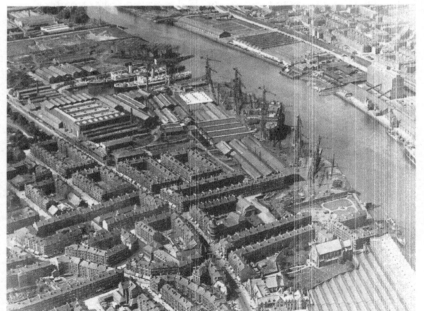

Govan from the air, 1930s: This aerial photo shows the dense mass of tenements around the shipyards at that time when it was 'three yairds' from Govan Cross to Shieldhall, Harland and Wolff, Fairfield's and Stephen's.

to Govan's limited green spaces. Lorne Street joins Pacific Drive at the interesting Four Winds building, one of the few structures of the former Prince's Dock still remaining here. Beyond lies the Glasgow Science Centre whilst straight ahead is found the Govan Town Hall. This grand building had a rather short life in the function for which it was constructed, being opened in 1901 to replace the earlier town hall, and operating as burgh headquarters for a mere 11 years till its functions were transferred to George Square in 1912, the year of Govan's annexation to Glasgow. Around the main entrance are busts of the local dignitaries of this period, while inside is a mosaic on the floor showing Govan's equally short-lived coat of arms, and motto *Nihil Sine Labore* (Nothing without Labour) – a slogan that reflects Govan's days of shipbuilding glory. Today the *umquile* Town Hall houses the offices and studios of Film City, a digital media centre. The former Clyde Navigation Trust's Govan graving docks lie a short distance on from the Burgh Hall. Here the Clyde-built ships were repaired and repainted for over a century, and the southernmost dock could take the biggest ships in the world, until the oil tanker era. On its closure in 1988, the docks area gradually became a wasteland of ruins. There were plans to turn the derelict docks into an upmarket housing development, a 'little Amsterdam' of flats, a hotel and floating restaurants. The ground was even cleared, but 25 years later nothing has happened. This would have been a wonderful place for a Clyde Maritime Museum, of which there was much talk in the 1990s. This idea was scuttled when, amongst other things, the Clyde-built *Britannia* (which was intended to be a star attraction) was instead, inexplicably and unjustifiably, located in Leith! Piracy – if not on the high seas, at least in high places. Glasgow and Clydeside's maritime generosity knows no bounds. First the *Cutty Sark*, started in Glasgow, finished in Dumbarton, was given to London, then the *Britannia* was taken by Edinburgh and in 2013 the former clipper *The Carrick*, aka *City of Adelaide*, was allowed to depart for its eponymous antipodean city. They should all have been part of a Clyde Maritime Museum that should have been here in Govan, and not for the desire for a better footfall, located as the Riverside Museum in Partick.

It might be said that Govan at least has the Glasgow Science Centre, located to the east of the former Prince's Dock. But, though in Govan, this aggregate of Science Centre, Imax Cinema, with the BBC Scotland and STV headquarters, is not of Govan. Hardly a soul from the district works there: the staff drive in and then out at the day's end

over the Squinty Bridge, and for Govanites this complex might as well
be on the moon.

Most people would – if they ever got there – hurry along Govan
road to Govan Cross, probably in their cars. And it is true there is a
lot of dereliction: empty buildings and waste ground where, behind
advertising hoardings, groups of men sit drinking by fires. But they
mind their business as I mind mine, and there is so much to see; you
have to be selective. Few of the tenements survive on the Govan Road,
but one that does draws the eye, the Cossar building (known after
John Cossar, who built it to house his printing works). He moved
here in 1890 after successfully establishing himself as the publisher of
the *Govan Chronicle* in 1875, followed by the *Govan Press* in 1878.
There are busts on the building of Burns and Scott, Scotland's two
greatest writers, and of the founders of printing, Caxton and Guten-
berg – and, just so that the big capitalists of the shipyards didn't have
a monopoly of immortalising themselves, busts of Mr and Mrs Cossar
as well. The firm closed down in 1983, as the rest of Govan's economy
contracted with the collapse of shipbuilding. Cossar published TCF
Brotchie's *The History of Govan* in 1905, when the area was at its
peak. Brotchie commented that nowhere in Govan were you out of
earshot of a hammer. A century later, most of them are silent.

Silent, too, is Highland Lane, down which thousands used to walk
to take the ferry from Govan to Finnieston until the mid-1970s. I
managed to catch one of the last of these on a trip to Ibrox in 1974,
and two of the crew – the workers on the Clyde ferries were collec-
tively known in the past as the Skye Navy – were chatting in Gaelic to
each other. A few years later, I was on a trip on the *Waverley* paddle
steamer and the same two guys were chatting to each other in Gaelic
on board that vessel whilst they plied the ropes. But the Skye Navy,
and the Clyde ferries, are no more.

Further along Govan Road on the right stood Napier House, built
in the Art Nouveau Glasgow style in 1899. It was one of the earliest
steel-framed buildings in the city, and the top floor was also Glasgow's first telephone exchange. Formerly used as a seamen's lodging
house, its occupants were latterly only doos which flew in and out of
the broken windows. The building was not beyond repair, but it was
demolished and an ugly hole now marks the spot.

Next comes a rather undistinguished social housing scheme from
the 1970s, on the site of the former Harland and Wolff shipyard: this
was the last to be built in Govan, and the first to close in 1962. Faced

with the prospect of Irish Home Rule, Harland and Wolff were planning to move their shipbuilding enterprises from Belfast to the Clyde, and this yard was laid out in 1912 on the sites of various other small shipbuilders, which Harland and Wolff bought out. When it opened the firm brought many workers across from Ulster and it is often stated that this increased the sectarian tensions in Govan, as these workers were all Protestant Unionists. In his autobiography *No Mean Fighter*, Harry MacShane says that no Catholic could expect to work in that yard. This statement is rather belied by the fact that he himself gained a job there in the 1950s, despite his name being a giveaway as to his background, and he further states that he had no problems with the largely Protestant foremen, and in fact was kept on when other workers were laid off because the timekeeper was a Catholic!

Just opposite the site of the Harland and Wolff yard is today found a fire station, which is on the site of the tenement where Sir Alex Ferguson, arguably Govan's greatest son, was brought up. Heading up Broomloan Road, past the original Govan Town Hall on the right which dates from the 1860s and has now been restored as workspaces, takes you past Broomloan Road School, sadly now a disintegrating ruin. This was Fergie's primary school. And yet further on you come to Ibrox Park, home of Rangers FC, where Ferguson plied his trade for a while as a player, albeit unhappily.[1] Ibrox is a Footballing Temple, the masterpiece of Archibald Leitch, civil engineer and architect – and Rangers supporter. The South Stand and its interior – A Listed – must be one of the grandest stadia anywhere. Outside stands a statue of John Grieg, a Rangers great, commemorating those killed in the disasters that have occurred over the years at Ibrox. Ibrox used to be the posh part of Govan, with a substantial middle-class population. Around the stadium can be found the terraces of the foremen, small businessmen and managers who formerly lived there; alas, these terraces are now some of the most neglected and run down housing in the whole of Govan.

It is an easy walk back to Walmer Crescent and the Subway from here, or gluttons for pavement punishment could hurry back to Govan Road where the fine Potted Heid building stands. This was a grand tenement built by a bank with ornate ironwork and granite pillars.

---

1 Readers interested in Ferguson and his Ibrox days can seek out the chapter 'Alex Ferguson's Govan' in my recent book, *A Glasgow Mosaic*. (2013).

It stood for many years in a desert of isolation but now has been surrounded by new housing developments filling the gaps.

By now we are at the heart of Govan, at the Cross. Two buildings especially catch the eye. One is Brechin's Bar, built in 1894 in Scots Baronial style. Ironically, it was originally the centre of Govan's Temperance Movement, and was known as the Cardell Hall, after its founder John Cardell. In the days when every street corner in Govan had a pub, another place you couldn't get a drink was the Pearce Institute, opened in 1906, a magnificent eclectic mix of Scottish and Dutch Renaissance architecture, with crow-step gables, oriel windows, external balconies, and a fully-rigged sailing ship (constructed by workers in the Fairfield yard.) Built by Rowand Anderson, the Institute was endowed by Lady Pearce in memory of her husband, a prime mover in the expansion of the Fairfield shipbuilding yard, of which he was at one time the owner. With its theatre, reading room and library, dining and recreation rooms, the Institute played a role in Govan social life till its sad closure a couple of years back. However, on the centenary of the beginnings of its construction in 1903, the Pearce Institute Regeneration Plan was launched, and the building has re-opened its doors as the 'Heart of Govan' once again. A large range of groups have already made the Pearce their home, including a couple of film companies and a wide variety of social and voluntary organisations.

Opposite the Institute is the statue known as the Black Man for its colouring; it depicts Pearce himself, who became Govan's first MP in 1885 – as a Conservative. Hailing from Kent, he moved to the Clyde from the naval dockyards at Chatham in the 1860s and by 1869 was the sole proprietor of Fairfields, becoming a millionaire before his death in 1888. Local legend has it that the Black Man looks around to see what is happening in Govan – or at least that's what the regulars at Brechin's Bar insist, usually around closing time.

The election of Pearce, the biggest local employer, as Govan's first MP illustrates an aspect of 19th-century life, the almost feudal power local capitalists wielded, albeit a democratic feudalism. Pearce was not unusual: many capitalists in Glasgow and elsewhere became local MPs – local provosts, councillors and JPs. In *Clydeside Capital 1870-1920*, Ronald Johnston calculated that in that period, 78 per cent of Glasgow councilors were capitalists, merchants and shipowners, and 30 per cent of the city's MPs were capitalists, with a large part of the rest made up by merchants, bankers, shipowners and the like. Political and economic powers were then almost transparently identical.

Though only about half of working-class males had the vote before 1918 in national elections (more had the vote in local elections), in Glasgow as elsewhere, it was not uncommon for many of these men at that time to vote for their employers. In a working-class area like Govan, Pearce must have been carried to Westminster largely on skilled workers' votes, and in 1910, when Labour first stood in Govan, they came third in what had become a Liberal seat. Govan, however, was one of the places where change began to be effected, and was an early Labour Party gain. It was the only Glasgow seat (apart from Gorbals) that the party won at the Khaki Election landslide of 1918, and was retained for the ILP by Neil Maclean thereafter. Even at the next Labour wipeout in 1931, Govan stayed with the ILP – though only by 600 votes. Govan has the distinction of being the first constituency in the UK to have elected a Muslim MP, Mohammed Sarwar for Labour in 1997.

When it was annexed by Glasgow in 1912, Govan was Scotland's fifth-biggest burgh, with a population of over 100,000, yet in the 1830s the population had been only 2,000. The growth, virtually unparalleled anywhere else in Scotland, was due almost entirely to Govan becoming the centre of the Scottish, British and indeed world, shipbuilding industry. Robert Napier opened his works in 1841, and was followed by John Elder, who in 1864 laid out his yard on the Fairfield farm, and others in turn followed him, such as Alexander Stephen at Linthouse. These yards built the Cunard liners and Atlantic cargo ships as well as warships. The long decline of the industry – which featured the famous Upper Clyde Shipbuilders work-in of the 1970s, when workers occupied the yards – led to the closing of most of the sites. But the Fairfield works – after going through as many name changes as a nuclear power station – survives today as BAE Systems, employing about 1,000 men, a shadow of its former self. At its wartime height, the shipbuilding industry in Govan employed 50,000.

Wages were high in the shipyards – at least for skilled men – but the working conditions were hard and dangerous. Housing – built quickly and speculatively– was generally squalid and overcrowded to a level we would find intolerable today – and it was no accident that it was in Govan that the housewives precipitated the Rent Strikes during the 1914–18 war. On the other hand, the paternalism of the Victorian employers was manifested in various ways. As well as the Pearce Institute mentioned, the Elder Park, which lies further along the Govan Road from the Pearce, was donated to the people of Govan in 1885 by Mrs Isabella Elder as a memorial to her husband. His statue (and hers) stands in the park. Elder rests his hand on the compound steam engine he developed and patented, which with its vast fuel savings gave the Clyde yards their competitive edge in Victorian times. Isabella also gave money to build the Elder Cottage Hospital and the Elder Park Library, opened by Andrew Carnegie in 1903. Inside the library are busts of John and Isabella Elder, reminding us that, as well as wealth, they sought immortality. Even streets in Govan bear the shipping magnates' names: Elder, Napier. Such paternalism immortalised its practitioners, but also provided social control; reading materials in these institutions was censored to choose materials 'edifying to the working classes' and only activities approved by the patrons could take place therein. In the PI men and women were separated for moral reasons, for example, they even had different entrances for the sexes!

Opposite the Elder Park, the men who were really Govan's greatest benefactors are commemorated in the statues at the entrance to Fairfields. These are a duo of anonymous shipyard workers carved in sandstone by Pittendrigh MacGillivray, an Aberdeen sculptor who did much work in Glasgow. MacGillivray was an early socialist, if of a somewhat eccentric nature, and clearly sympathised with his subject. He attended meetings of William Morris' Socialist League in Glasgow in the 1880s. The Shipwright and Engineer are real-life manual workers, a break with Victorian habits of representing the trades by idealised classical maidens, cherubs or, at best, workers in the garb of medieval trades. The figures express the pride and confidence of the skilled and educated working men who were Govan's backbone for 150 years. MacGillivray was paid £250 for the work in 1890. The only other comparable work I know of is Lavery's *Shipbuilding on the Clyde* in the City Chambers, where a fine mural shows men at work in a shipyard c.1888. This was a one-off for Lavery, a society painter whose subjects were usually a world away from working-class life, and was a commission for the then Glasgow Corporation.

In *Glasgow in 1901*, written for the Glasgow exhibition of that year, James Hamilton Muir (a composite name for the three people who produced the book) draws a picture of the Glasgow working man, and sets him in Govan. He is called John MacMillan, a fitter, and is seen as the new working man; interested in football, and a Rangers supporter. 'The best you can say for football is that it has given the working man a topic for conversation,' state the authors, for their imaginary typical worker is non-political. He lives in a room and kitchen and goes 'doon the watter' for his holidays:

When his time was served he became a Union man, and thought all the world of his district delegate. He stauns up for himsel, not only against the common enemy, his employer, but also against his comrades in the allied trades if they invade his frontiers.

Despite being rather a caricature, there is a truth in this picture, as in most caricatures – a picture of what Lenin would have described as 'trades union consciousness'. Against this, the authors draw a cameo of the minority of workers, whom they call the backbone of the working class, and describe them as 'radical and Calvinist by inheritance and tradition'. This type of worker ignores football and is teetotal, and 'his discussions are political and theological... and though his active interest in Calvinism may have abated, its principles still control his conduct'.

Here we have the working-class minority, some of whom would become leaders of Red Clydeside, with the John MacMillans following them for their own economic aims, and some of whom would add a more Orange colour to the waters of the proletarian river.

It is fitting that with their rich history, the Govan yards would feature prominently in one of the last great battles of the Glasgow industrial working class, the Upper Clyde Shipbuilders' (UCS) work-in of the early 1970s. The UCS campaign led to the biggest explosion of class struggle in Glasgow since the days of Red Clydeside. The decision of the Heath Government to withhold credits for yards that had full order books led to a work-in, organised mainly by shop stewards influenced by the Communist Party, and centred on Govan. Indeed, its most prominent and eloquent leader was Jimmy Reid, born and bred in Govan. Against those who argued that the UCS work-in could be a catalyst for a general strike to bring down the Government, the shop stewards' committee waged a broad and moderate campaign, which drew widespread sympathy. Those who had expected the revolution were disappointed. As one worker replied to a speaker arguing for a general strike, 'That's no in ma union rule book'. When told that a simple work-in would lead to defeat the worker replied, 'Defeat? Ah'm used tae that son. Ah'm a Partick Thistle supporter'.

In June 1971, 100,000 people struck work in support of the workers occupying their yards, and 40,000 demonstrated in George Square; in August the numbers of those taking industrial action reached 200,000 – and 80,000, the biggest demonstration in Glasgow for over 50 years, took to the streets. Faced with this, the Government partially backed down, and a compromise was eventually reached, which maintained – for a time – 8,500 jobs. In Govan itself, Fairfields remained open but the Stephen's yard closed, following Harland and Wolff, which had already shut in 1962. The distance between Govan Cross and the Southern General Hospital was no longer 'three yairds,' but a single one. And there is talk now that BAE Systems may centralise its warship production in Scotstoun further downriver and close Fairfields, ending 175 years of shipbuilding in Govan.

We have missed out something, one of Govan's greatest glories, about which few in Glasgow are aware, despite its world-historic significance. When getting to know Glasgow on foot 40 years ago, I entered the graveyard of Govan Old Parish Church to look at the gravestones, dating back to the 17th century, and to pre-industrial Govan. Finding the building open, I went in and found that the best was actually inside. I discovered that there had been a Christian church here from at least the sixth century, well before Glasgow Cathedral was built, and that the present kirk, designed by Rowand Anderson (architect of the Pearce Institute) was at least the fourth to be built on the site. The history of the kirk since the Reformation throws up, amongst others, the ministries of Andrew Melville (1577–80), architect of the Presbyterian structure of the Church of Scotland and George Macleod (1930–8), whose experiences of Govan in the depression helped him to found the Iona Community dedicated to world peace and justice.

But even more remarkable are the collection of carved stones in the kirk, one of the most important collections of early Christian sculpture in Scotland. These were all carved locally from sandstone by skilled Govan craftsmen, showing that, 1,000 years before the glories of shipbuilding, Govan had another glory period as a wealthy community. Amongst the sculptures, around 30 in all, are the stunning hogback burial stones, possibly from the tenth century and of Norse-influenced origin, many burial slabs and shafts combining Christian and pre-Christian motifs, and most amazing of all, the carved stone Govan Sarcophagus. This was originally assumed to be the burial coffin of St Constantine, but is now thought to be of a later date. One fascinating feature of this is the hole in the base, which allowed the decomposing matter from the body to drain out of the coffin.

Monies have come from Historic Scotland and elsewhere to help with interpretation and publicity of the church's treasures, in an effort to boost visitor numbers. Any Glaswegian who has not visited here should be ashamed of themselves, and any visitor to the city should head for Govan to see the most interesting ecclesiastical building in Glasgow. (www.govanold.org.uk)

Elder Park, Govan's green lung, cannot claim to be one of Glasgow's most beautiful dear green spaces. However, as well as hosting the fine JJ Burnet Elderpark Library, which Govanites will proudly tell you was constructed before any of Glasgow's local public libraries, it contains an interesting collection of public sculptures, for which a Heritage Trail has been written and which is available in the library. Once past the park and the long wall of the Fairfield yard, you are in quite a distinct part of Govan; Linthouse. This area was dominated by the Stephen's shipyard, and has a very fine collection of surviving red sandstone tenements, clustered round Linthouse Church, which has many associations with the Stephens family. Like Pearce, the original Stephen was an outsider, from Aberdeen, who saw that the days of sail were over and moved to the Clyde to build with steam. The offices of the yard are still extant, serving as workspaces down in Holmfauld Road, but the glory of Stephens was its engine shop, dubbed the Palace of Victorian Engineering, which was dismantled and re-assembled at the Maritime Museum in Irvine. I have nothing against Irvine, but – why Irvine? Why not somewhere in Glasgow? Charity may be greater than Faith or Hope, but sometimes it should begin at home. The LUV (Linthouse Urban Village) café here at the north-west corner of Elder Park, where the Govan Road meets Drive Road, is a welcome stop for refreshment before proceeding further.

A fitting addition to any Govan perambulation is a trip further west along the Renfrew Road to the site of the former SCWS complex at Shieldhall. Many Govanites worked till its closure in this, one of the largest industrial concerns in Glasgow. At its height, 6,000 people turned out footwear, furniture and foodstuffs in a whole village of factories for the chain of Co-op retail stores throughout Glasgow and Scotland. In the space left derelict since its closure, a modern village could easily be built. John Hume in his excellent *Industrial Archeology of Glasgow* (1974) is a bit sniffy about the SCWS site, saying that 'the buildings are mainly distinguished by their number'. Actually they include one of the finest industrial buildings in Glasgow. The Luma Co-op light bulb factory, now converted to offices and flats, is a splendid art-deco sight as one enters Glasgow from the motorway on the west. If you go and visit the former factory, now restored as flats, you will find behind it a cluster of art-deco cottages, imaginatively built by the local housing association in the style of the Luma works.

The Co-op was probably the most important organisation in working-class life till the 1950s. Many more were members of the Co-op than of political parties or even of trade unions. Roughly half of Glasgow's population were Co-op members between the wars (it used to be said that when the revolution came, you would be spared if you could remember your Co-op number). The Co-op provided cheaper staples of life for working-class people, the possibility of credit at non-usurious rates, and the divvi, which financed luxury purchases. The Co-op also provided employment, not only at Shieldhall but in its mass of outlet stores, in good conditions. Further, for a lucky few, it provided good housing above its tenement premises, or at Shieldhall. Working-class loyalty to the Co-ops was intense if occasionally irreverent:

I like a sassidge, a Cooperative sassidge
Though ye cannae get near it for the smell
If ye fry it wi an ingan, ye'll hear the ingan singan
'Mary ma Scots Blue Belle'.

The factory is reached by going along Renfrew Road past the Sufferin (Southern) General Hospital, after passing the site of the former Stephen's shipyard. Walking down Bogmoor Road gives you an impression of the immensity of these works, and the Luma factory with its cottages – the only relics of this once-mighty effort at economic Co-operation – is found at the head of Hardgate Road. John Maclean was active in the Co-operative movement, which he saw both as a school for socialism and as a method of waging the class struggle. He foresaw

Co-operative Works, Shieldhall circa 1910: A fine drawing of the Co-op complex at Shieldhall, one of the biggest of its kind in Europe. It produced a wide variety of manufactured goods for distribution in the Co-op stores.

the expansion of Co-operative production alongside the increasing concentration of capitalist concerns and argued to the Scottish Co-operative Conference in 1911 that:

> Working men's Co-operation is within sight of a desperate struggle with capitalists' trusts. When the ultimate struggle between the huge trusts and Co-operation takes place, it will be a fight between capital and labour.

The former SCWS site is currently the scene of a massive project that will result in the construction of the largest building in Scotland – a new hospital. Even this will only occupy a part of the former SCWS site, and one considers; where once thousands productively worked, soon thousands of sick people will receive treatment. The idea appears to be that the Southern General (initially constructed as the Govan Poorhouse) might be converted into the kind of housing that professional people might consider, leading to a return of a middle class in the area. Certainly over the last five years much social housing and so-called 'affordable' housing has been constructed in the heart of Govan, leading to an enormous improvement in the look of the area. Nothing is more demoralising than wasteland. This improvement has been aided by projects such as the £2 million spent upgrading the public realm amenities in the area round Govan Cross, and the restoration of the Aitken cast iron fountain there.

A fitting end to a visit to Govan is to stroll to the Elder Park Library where the Govan Heritage Exhibition will elaborate on some of the things you have seen and point to others you may have missed. (Check on opening hours: 0141 445 1047). Then it is a short walk to the Govan Cross Underground and transport back to wherever you started from – or, as I usually do, you can retrace the walk back to Cessnock for just one more look at, and possibly to finally get that perfect photograph of, Walmer Crescent.

People who value their heritage value their communities and also themselves. And the folk of Govan still do value their heritage, despite the economic ravages that have beset the area in the last 40 years. Who, even in Glasgow, knows that the city's oldest procession is the Govan Fair, established by Govan's weavers in 1756? (Glasgow People's Palace, by the way, hosts a banner borne by the Govan Weavers when they fought at Sheriffmuir against the Jacobites in 1715). Every year in June thousands line the streets to watch as the Govan Queen proceeds through the 'burgh,' preceded by the Glasgow Police Pipe Band, two mounted policemen, and the whole parade headed by a bearer, traditionally a ship's joiner, bearing a sheep's heid. The sheep's heid represents the story of when a Govan minister forbade his servant girl from marrying a local lad; the lad eloped with the girl and decapitated all the minister's sheep into the bargain. The day of the Govan Fair is also marked by various well-supported sporting and other events. While there are still ghettoes in Govan that would make a grown man weep, there is much more to this area than Rab C and the Rangers. And for the first time in many, many decades, it is possible to be optimistic that the district faces a better future.

For Govan Old Church see www.govanold.org.uk or
0141 440 2466
For the Pearce Institute www.pearceinstitute.org or
0141 445 6007

CHAPTER FIVE

Clydebank: A Cut Above

THERE ARE PLACES adjoining Glasgow that are not Glasgow. Paisley is an example. With their 800-year independent history, the Buddies are not Glaswegians. They have a different culture, expressing itself in things like a softer humour than Glasgow's, and a proverbial meanness. On the other hand, there are places bordering the city that, despite the fact that Glasgow's boundaries exclude them, are in every respect Glaswegian – and one of them is Clydebank. It is even surrounded by Glasgow, except to the west, and if ever the boundaries of the conurbation are redrawn logically, it will be a part of the city, of which it is simply a western extension.

I worked in Clydebank at the Technical College for 22 years, teaching history. Before I got the job I knew nothing of the town, though I remembered reading an article about the place in *The Guardian* at the time of the UCS work-in of 1971–2. This was to the effect that places like Clydebank, with their 19th-century industries and slums, had no place in modern Britain. Never let the truth (for example, that for most of the 19th century, Clydebank didn't even exist) stand in the way of good newspaper copy. The writer did not actually advocate bringing back the Luftwaffe to finish the job Hitler started in the 1940s, but clearly supported the then Conservative Government's policy of killing so-called lame ducks – as they saw shipbuilding. But the town didn't just produce ships, it produced people. And it didn't want to disappear, either.

The best way to start a daunder round Clydebank is to do what I did many times for 22 years: take the train from Glasgow to Singer station. This used to be Kilbowie station and was renamed when the American Singer sewing-machine company moved its factory here from Bridgeton in Glasgow in the 1880s. By 1890 Singer's employed 6,000 people at what was one of the largest factories in the world. A siding was built off Singer station to take the special trains that carried thousands of workers from Glasgow to Singer's daily, though many families moved west with the factory. At the college I taught everything from 17 year olds to 70 year olds. One of the latter told me his grandfather had moved to Clydebank from Bridgeton with Singer's. The

Clydebank

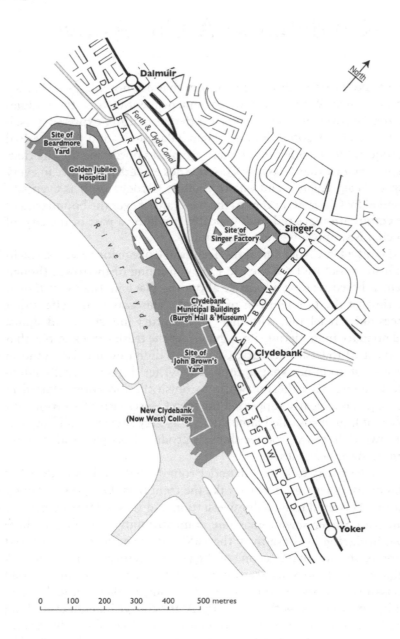

Clydebank Route Summary

1. Take a train to Yoker and walk along the Glasgow Road, passing the site of the John Brown & Company shipyard (its Titan Crane is open to visitors) and the new West College Scotland's Clydebank Campus.

2. Continue past the Clydebank Town Hall and the library to Dalmuir.

3. Pick up the Forth and Clyde Canal towpath/walkway back east, passing on the left (north) side the huge site of the former Singer factory.

4. At Kilbowie Road, head up past the shopping complexes to Singer station, and home. (Alternatively, take the Bankie Trek to Carbeth (see website details on page 76).

Approximate route time: 2.5 hours

high point of Singer's was in the 1950s, when with 17,000 workers it was the largest industrial unit in Europe. Even in the '70s, when I went to Clydebank, Singer's employed 6,500 people.

Singer's was one of the first factories to apply mass-production techniques, described by John Maclean in *Justice* (1911), the national paper of the Social Democratic Federation:

> There are 41 departments and the various processes have been so divided and sub-divided that few outside the office staff will know how many stages the wood, iron and steel have to go through before the machine is completed. All except a few engineers, moulders and joiners, are tied down to work no longer skilled.

Only these skilled workers were unionised. The works saw the most important strike in the west of Scotland before the outbreak of First World War. Three thousand women at the factory came out in 1911, trying to form a trade union and looking for increased wages. They were followed by the unskilled and largely non-unionised male workers, the leading activists amongst whom belonged to the Socialist Labour Party (SLP), a Marxist group advocating industrial unionism (One Big Union).

Unfortunately the men in the engineering union, the ASE, did not come out in support and the strike was eventually defeated in the face

Singer Strike 1911: Workers leaving the huge Singer factory during the period of the 1911 strike, when the company employed over 10,000 people and still had a huge clock that was visible for miles around. Note the railway siding into the actual factory.

of a management threat to sack the strikers. Maclean publicised the strike in *Justice*, in a series of articles. He stated:

> If the ranks are held unbroken, if discipline is maintained and if the committee is firm in attitude and unanimous in spirit and objective and tactics, then in the state of present trade, the trust will have, for the time being at least, to yield to the strikers.

And he blamed the ultimate defeat after two weeks on 'the lack of feeling of class solidarity'. The SLP men who had managed to get the unskilled workers out in support of the women were sacked after the strike.

If Singer's came from Glasgow to Clydebank, so too did the shipyards. A decade or so before the Singer's move, Thomson's shipyard had left Govan and moved to the area, again bringing many of its workers with it (at first daily by paddle steamer from Govan, till their housing was constructed). Thomson's also brought the name Clydebank, which the town subsequently took from the shipyard itself. At first Thomson's built paddle steamers, and later transatlantic liners, such as *The City of New York*. John Brown's, the Sheffield steelmasters, took over the yard in 1899 and expanded it to build larger ships. From less than 1,000 people, Clydebank had grown to 30,000 by 1900.

These two industrial units dominated employment in the town, but others from Glasgow followed, and a large part of the incoming population originated from the city. Clydebank was the East Kilbride of its day, a Glasgow overspill. Between the shipyard by the river and the Singer factory up the brae, the fields were filled with tenements. These were tight-packed and in 1936, 40 per cent of the housing was officially overcrowded, one of the highest figures in Scotland.

From the dilapidated Singer station you look out over Clydebank Business Park, which occupies the site of the former works, and this gives an idea of its vast scale. I remember coming back after the college summer holiday in 1980 and looking over to the hills of Renfrew, which I hadn't seen from Clydebank before. Puzzled, I realised Singer's had been demolished during the summer. The Singer Tower, with its four eight-metre-diameter clocks, once claimed to be the biggest timepieces in the world, had already gone by the time I started at the college. This was a magic clock, since from the inexhaustible metal of its hands every family in Clydebank has at least one ashtray. Another amazing Bankie fact is that it had the highest concentration of piano ownership in Britain. When the Blitz insurance claims went in, it was found that almost every close had boasted eight of them, one in each flat, though sadly all the evidence was destroyed!

The railway bounded Singer's to the north. If you walk down Kilbowie Road from the station, you come to the now reopened Forth and Clyde Canal, which was the factory's southern boundary. Reclamation and restoration has created a pleasant walk along the south bank of the canal for a bit under a mile, till it crosses with Dumbarton Road. The canal carries on from here to Old Kilpatrick, with interesting protected wetlands and salt flats under the Erskine Bridge. Thereafter it leads in a couple of miles to its outlet at Bowling Docks, where the old berthings and custom house are well worth a visit. But let's stay with the Bankies for the moment.

This part of Clydebank is called Dalmuir and some local residents think it isn't really Clydebank. Dalmuir mainly exists because William Beardmore built a shipyard here in the early 1900s. When it closed, this left a huge asbestos dump in the site, uncovered. The local council seized on a proposal for a private hospital for part of the site, both to bring jobs during the mass unemployment of the 1980s, and as a way of capping the site – for which they didn't have the cash. So the UHI Hospital was built, a miracle, state-of-the-art building, which was supposed to treat rich patients from the Gulf States and elsewhere.

Advertising materials offered helicopter flights from Glasgow airport to the UHI, to potential patients who were not told about the asbestos. Instead the brochures showed pictures of Loch Lomond as the hospital's (implied) location. A hotel, ironically called Beardmore's, was built for the prospective guests of these sick fat cats. Never more than a third full and surviving on NHS custom, the place was bought for the NHS in the 1990s – after having largely been paid for by public money in the first place. True to their radical traditions, the Bankies fought long and hard against the private hospital, but at least now it is treating some of the people who paid for it. The former UHI is now known as the Golden Jubilee Hospital.

For Clydebank has always been a very political place, possibly the most political in Scotland. In 1922, Davie Kirkwood was elected for the ILP, the only Red Clydesider elected from outwith the city boundaries, proving again that Clydebank is really Glasgow. And between the wars Clydebank became one of the power bases of the Communist Party, based largely on the shipyards, or on John Brown's, the daddy of them all, which at its wartime maximum employed 10,000 workers. Turning back east along Dumbarton Road from Dalmuir, you come to one end of the site of the former Brown's yard, but you have to walk a very long way, the best part of a mile, before you come to the other end of what was possibly British shipbuilding's greatest yard. Unlike the Fairfields yard in Govan, 'Broon's' management and office block was notable only for its size, and was without architectural merit. Nothing of it remains.

A fine 'Head of a Shipyard Worker' sculpture was erected in 1992 opposite the former main gate of the yard, and on a part of the cleared site by the river is found the re-located Clydebank (now West) College. The rest of the site of the former yard was to have been occupied by a private housing development, but almost a decade later, not a brick has been laid. The huge Titan crane, built for Brown's by William Arrol and a masterpiece of Scottish industrial engineering, has been restored as a hoped-for visitor attraction at the far end of the desolate and windy wasteland.

Where does one start with this yard? Brown's built the *Lusitania*, whose sinking in 1915 helped bring the USA into First World War. It built the *Queen Mary* in the 1930s, which signaled hope at a time when 50 per cent of the town's workers were unemployed. And it built the *Queen Elizabeth II* in the booming 1960s, when unemployment and capitalist crises were supposed to be things of the past. The yard

was, with Fairfields in Govan, one of the main focal points of the
UCS work-in, and the power base of its main spokesman Jimmy Reid,
though he was a Govanite, not a Bankie. Like many of the leaders
of the work-in, Reid was a member of the Communist Party, and in
its aftermath stood for Parliament in Clydebank as a Workers' Candidate, getting a solid 5,000 votes. For a while the former Brown's
yard operated, building oil rigs with a reduced work force, for various
owners. The engineering side of the business continued with about
1,500 men until 1997, when closure ended 'Broon's' last link with
the town.

Something I liked about Clydebank was the low profile of sectarianism, and this despite the fact that a good third of the population
came from Ireland (from both sides of the fence). The solidly left-
wing nature of the place helped to dampen this division, and I can
honestly say I never came across the problem in the college, except
from one pupil, who was not from Clydebank, and who wrote an
essay about Prodesens and Kafflicks full of the usual nonsense. As
well as history, I taught apprentices something called social studies.
These were guys from the trades and factories, with many coming
from the shipyards, and teaching them was really hard work, but
often rewarding. And even in the general debate and banter, you
could always tell the Bankies; they were just that bit sharper, that bit
more informed, than the others.

Brown's was always half-hidden by the tenements along Dumbarton Road, and also by the civic buildings of the Burgh. Much as I love
the Bankies, I am not going to claim their town as a Venice or Athens,
or Rome of the North. Clydebank's main asset is its people, rather than
its buildings. But it has the usual cluster of civic buildings, attractive
enough, if not outstanding. These consist of the Town Hall, the library,
the former baths and Public washhouse, and the Clydebank Museum,
which hosts the world's largest collection of sewing machines. Singer
deposited examples of their new models as they appeared, many of
them things of real beauty. The model 15k (called after Kilbowie) sold
20 million up to 1962 when production ended, and everyone's mother
used to have one of these finely-detailed black-cast machines, the older
ones with the treadle, the newer ones electric. So if sewing machines
are your religion, Clydebank is your Mecca.

In the appropriately named Agamemnon (he was a character in one
of Aeschylus's plays as well as Homer's *Iliad*) Street off Dumbarton
Road used to be situated the Clydebank Repertory Theatre, established

in 1943, where many of Scotland's actors first trod the boards, including Russell Hunter. By the time I was going there in the '70s and early '80s, the boards were distinctly spongy with the rot, the smell of which infested the building, but the performances were still good. Before that in the 1920s, there were the Clydebank Players, a thespian offshoot of the ILP, and the Clarion Players and Workers' Theatre Group also performed in the burgh regularly between the wars. And this place, which the Guardian thought ought not to exist, also produced possibly the finest (after Glasgow's Orpheus) amateur choir in the West of Scotland, the Clydebank Lyric, the selling of whose tickets was the periodic duty in the College of relatives of performers. When the Red Army Choir or the Moscow State Circus would come to town, busloads of Bankies could be guaranteed to attend. See Kulcher, see the Bankies.

But that does not end what these folk produced. John Brown's yard was not only a crucible of politics and trades unionism, but also of what was possibly Scotland's most important mountaineering club, the Creag Dhu. In the '30s Depression, many workers were unemployed, and they used their time to good effect by working out means of getting to the hills and mountains around Glasgow. They thus established the tradition of the working-class mountaineer, in a sport previously the preserve of the gentleman climber. Andy Sanders, the founder of the Creag Dhu, was a Brown's man, and the widening of his horizons and ambitions in the hills had the ultimate result of grooming him for the post of general manager at the yard. And there was Carbeth, of which more later.

There are little bits and pieces of architecture in Clydebank, cameos of pre-1914 styles that are worth a look if you ferret them out. Just east of Brown's yard was the marshaling depot of the Caledonian Railway Company, and there can be found a couple of the cottages they built for their employees, with the company logo and other sandstone reliefs on the walls, although that railway line is no more. Back on Dumbarton Road is the quaintly named Kizil Mansions, a rather superior tenement in an Art Nouveau style, which survived the Blitz. It should be remembered that much of Clydebank was destroyed in the Second World War, when only eight houses totally escaped damage.

One third of the 12,000 houses were totally destroyed and the rest damaged to varying degrees, and 500 people were killed in the raids of 1941. The worst damage was to the working-class tenement areas around the shipyard. North of Brown's, heading back towards the canal, there is little housing left, only a mess of roads, warehouses and a ghastly theme-park-style pool, which was another private but publicly funded venture that went bankrupt and had to be taken over by the local authority. The kind of place where you paddle and eat burgers.

Before we arrive back at Kilbowie Road, there is a huge shopping centre that, along with the Business Park, helped the town in the jobs sphere when the worst of the '80s industrial closures were taking place. The canal here sports (so they say) the world's only floating fish and chip shop, McMonagles, serving the delicacy from a purpose-built static boat on the canal. As I said before, Clydebank isn't Venice. On Kilbowie Road, you can look up and down its sweep and realise what the Blitz did to the town; elsewhere you would blame the planners, but here they had their work done for them. Back at Singer's, to your right behind some houses is yet another shopping development. This was formerly the ground of Clydebank FC, which they sold to pay debts, but were then unable to find another home. The team now plays in junior football, which is a reflection of the way events have hit the town.

But the Bankies are nothing if not resilient. The population of the burgh has fallen from over 50,000 to under 40,000 with Dalmuir in the last 25 years. While the new local jobs are often low paid and unskilled, many of the skilled men in Clydebank refused to give up. The town has the greatest average drive to work distance of any in Scotland, and as well as this, many Bankies got jobs in North Sea oil, commuting during the week to Aberdeen, or overseas to areas where their skills were in demand, like the Middle East. What Nazism couldn't kill, Thatcherism didn't either. Even the *Clydebank Press*, founded in 1891, still comes out every week, though now named the *Clydebank Post*.

UCS Work-in poster, 1971: One of the better pieces of propaganda for the UCS work-in that had a stronghold in John Brown's Clydebank yard. Brown's was one of the slimmed-down parts of UCS which survived, though it, too, eventually closed in the 1990s.

At Singer station you can catch a train back to Glasgow. Or you can take the Bankie Trek, which I have written about elsewhere.[1] In the 1930s, many families in Clydebank had huts at a place called Carbeth, about ten miles north of the town. These had developed from tents established on a sympathetic landowner's estate pre-First World War, the huts gradually extending to a village of over 100. As well as the huts, the Carbeth residents built a swimming pool by damming a burn. And there was a wee shop run by Jimmy Robinson, a fanatical communist, who always had a brew, day or night, for arrivals. This was their weekend and holiday escape, a socialist Butlin's, whose atmosphere is described in Glaser's *Growing Up in the Gorbals*, in the chapter 'A Taste of Freedom':

> Talk was of politics, of jobs and apprenticeships, of sex and conquest except when girls were in the party. Those summer nights were not really endless and totally wonderful but they seemed to be. Arrivals in the night were uniquely wonderful, filled with a sense of homecoming to a place where your lungs drew in new air that was your very own. Fellowship of the night. A time for innocents.

Though people like Glaser came from the Gorbals, most of the hutters were from Clydebank. They had no cars so the Bankies walked, up Kilbowie Road, over the Kilpatrick Hills, and then down into Carbeth. (Now you can get a bus from Singers to Faifley, Clydebank's post-war housing estate, and save a couple of miles walking.) During the Blitz, when the initial air-raid provision for the folk of the town was appalling, many had to spend nights in the open on the Kilpatrick Hills without food or shelter. Those with huts at Carbeth decamped there with their children, and the men walked to the shipyards and factories on Monday morning. You can follow this walk, and find more about the Carbeth experience, at this web address:

www.glasgowwestend.co.uk/people/ianmitch.html

From the Kilpatrick Hills you overlook Clydebank's Auchentoshan Distillery, producer of Scotland's best Lowland malt, which advertises itself as 'Glasgow's Whisky'. This proves my point. What a Bankie distillery does, a Buddy one would never do.

---

1 In the chapter 'Walking in and out of Town' in my *Walking through Scotland's History*, (2007).

CLYDEBANK: A CUT ABOVE

    For a while I went back to Clydebank to do the occasional
Workers' Educational Association class – or Wrinklies Educational
Association, as it should be, since those attending were all well over
70. And they were all women, for the men were dead. Some, in their
'80s, had lost their men in the war, others' husbands had died from
asbestosis or from the problems associated with a region where male
life-expectancy is generally low. And they had all either been to Carbeth,
or knew people in the Creag Dhu, or were members of the Rep or the
Lyric, or had a trade union or political background, or any combina-
tion of these. They called me 'son' and bought my books, though a few
of them could not really afford to, so they got a reduction. And they
reminded me that some of the best folk who ever trod this earth were
the politicised generation of working-class people who came out of the
struggles of the first half of the 20th century. They were always a
minority of their fellows, even in a place like Clydebank. But the
Bankie of the species was just that wee cut above the rest.
    However, nobody is perfect. In the 1970s, Clydebank successfully
campaigned against incorporation into Glasgow, and for a while had
its own council. But they paid the price for this in the 1990s, when
another local government reorganisation put them in West Dunbartonshire, instead of being a part of the City of Culture where they
belong. After the Depression, the Blitz and Thatcherism, they deserve
better. So I have annexed them into Glasgow for my book. I can pay
them no greater compliment.

CHAPTER SIX

Yoker and Scotstoun: Siamese Twins

FOR THE 22 YEARS I worked in Clydebank, I went each day through Yoker and Scotstoun. Sometimes by bus along Dumbarton Road, sometimes by train between Glasgow and Clydebank. And many times I cycled by the designated track on the bed of an old railway that bisected the district. There is no part of the city whose physical imagery is so fixed in my mind as this composite 'Yokerstoun'. Give me a pen and pencil, and from my mental map I could probably produce a pretty accurate street plan and building description of the whole area. In addition, many of my students, both the industrial apprentices and those seeking to gain qualifications for university entry, came from Yokerstoun.

It is a district where pavement pedestrianism might appear to be unpromising. It is not that it is Glasgow's most deprived region – far from it. There are parts of Yoker especially that are abrasive, but nothing like Dalmarnock or Possil is to be found in the Yokerstoun area. No, it is something else. Both these areas were new ones, which grew up from virtually nothing a century or so ago, and they did not overlay much of previous historical significance. In terms of its built environment, Yokerstoun does not possess many of the qualities that made Glasgow Britain's premier Victorian city. Springburn, for example, is of world historical architectural significance, when compared to Yokerstoun – everything being relative. What makes this area an essential component of any book that deals with working-class industrial Glasgow, is its role in the history of the working-class movement, especially around the time of the First World War. From that perspective primarily does Yoker – and Scotstoun – gain great importance.

Where they meet, like Siamese twins joined at the head, these districts contain two of the historically most important industrial units on Clydeside: Albion Motors in Scotstoun and the adjacent Yarrows shipyard stretching into Yoker. To those who like to brand Glasgow's industry as '19th-century,' it needs to be pointed out that both of these factories date from the 20th. The Alfred Yarrows shipyard moved from the Thames to the Clyde in 1906, whilst Albion Motors, mainly a commercial vehicle producer, had opened a couple of years earlier. These were not dinosaurs of the Industrial Revolution, but the highest-tech industries of their day – and for many years to follow. Along with Weirs in Cathcart and the Parkhead Forge, these two factories were the main centres of industrial unrest in the years 1914–19, the key power bases of the Clyde Workers' Committee (CWC). Formerly, a railway served these and other industrial units along the Clyde. The closure of this and construction of a cycle track on its bed has provided a convenient vantage point for a traverse of Yokerstoun on a high belvedere.

Invisible to the naked eye, Scotstoun starts where Dumbarton Road meets Victoria Park Drive South, and Methil Street is the border. Leaving Whiteinch, the cycle track goes parallel to the south of Earl Street, which itself lies south of Dumbarton Road. Interesting collections of English-style cottages are seen to the left of the cycle track. Called the Harland Cottages, they have nothing to do with Harland and Wolff, as local lore would have you believe, despite the latter firm owning a works hereabouts (later sold to Albion Motors). The cottages were built in 1895, many years before Harland took over the former Coventry armaments factory of South Street in the 1920s. Subsequently Windsor Street changed its name to Harland Street and the cottages followed suit. They face across South Street to the location of the former Connell's shipyard, whose undistinguished brick offices can still be identified.

The platforms of the former Scotstoun East station, where the workers of Albion and Yarrows detrained, are still clearly visible at the sides of the cycle track. Now a car park lies to the south of this; and across South Street itself is what remains of Albion Motors, the former bus and truck manufacturer. This plant once covered the whole area around the junction of South and Balmoral Streets, now either derelict or warrened with Third World cowboy capitalists. After becoming part of British Leyland in 1951, then DAF motors in the 1980s, then experiencing a management buyout in the '90s, 'the Albion' still survives as American Axle and Manufacturing (AAM) with about 400 workers, making axles and transmission equipment for commercial vehicles. AAM faced a three-month strike in 2008 at their Detroit plant by 4,500 workers when they attempted to cut wages from $28 to $14 an hour, which is nearer to what they pay in Glasgow. A trip to the Glasgow Riverside Museum shows you the gorgeous commercial vehi-

Yoker and Scotstoun

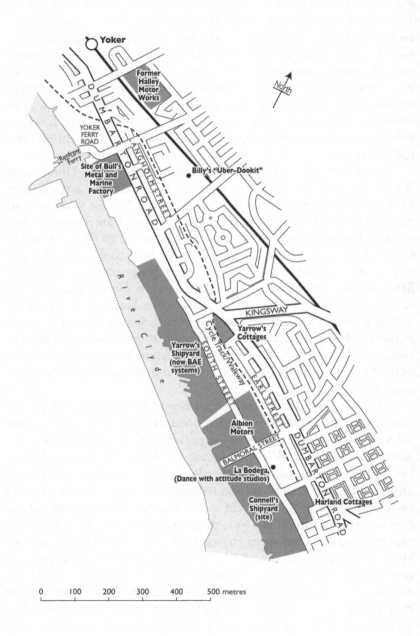

Yoker and Scotstoun Route Summary

1   Take a train to Yoker station.

2   Walk back along Dumbarton Road through Yoker until you reach the Kingsway (Yarrow's houses).

3   Head down to South Street and past Yarrow's (BAE Systems) into an increasingly post-apocalyptic industrial landscape. By the time you come to the Dance with Attitude studios, you will be seeking refreshment!

4   Continue to the Harland Cottages, then by fair means or foul gain the cycle track on the old railway just to the north.

5   Head back west along this excellent belvedere till you regain Yoker and a plethora of dookits, amongst which Billy's is the best.

6   The cycle track goes under Dumbarton Road, but you want to regain that thoroughfare at some point and return to Yoker station.

Approximate route time: 2.5 hours

cles, all with the distinctive Albion rising sun badge, which used to pour out of these works when they employed many thousands of men.

One of the men they employed was Willie Gallacher, author of *Revolt on the Clyde* (1936). Though starting life as a Paisley Buddy, and later becoming the Communist MP for West Fife, Gallacher's political apprenticeship was served in Glasgow. He worked at the Albion on various occasions, until he was sacked after being imprisoned and jailed in 1916 for his part in the fight against wartime conscription. Gallacher became shop stewards' convener at the Albion and later chairman of the Clyde Workers' Committee. Though he might exaggerate his overall importance in the events of Red Clydeside, there is little doubting Gallacher's role in helping to organise the men at the Albion in support of the Rent Strikes in Glasgow during the war. He also helped to break the isolation of the Weir's Strike in 1915, turning it into one of national importance. The stewards at Albion:

> ... decided on action with Weir's and called a mass meeting. We also got in touch with Yarrow's and Mechan's to ensure they also took action. The delegation of the Albion, of which I was

the leader, arrived at St Mungo Hall... I said that I brought greetings from the Albion and a pledge of solidarity as long as the fight lasted. I told them that Yarrow's and Mechan's were on the move. What a scene there was as they jumped to their feet and cheered.

Gallacher added in his book that 'The workers of the Clyde had broken through the rotten atmosphere of war jingoism'. In fact, he and his fellow Socialist Labour Party shop stewards avoided criticism of the war in their industrial capacities and concentrated on economic issues, like wages and the dilution of labour. For this, they were criticised by John Maclean, who always put opposition to the war at the forefront on any agitation. But for all his faults, there was worse than Willie Gallacher, and after he died in his council flat in 1965 in his native Paisley, 40,000 Buddies followed the coffin or lined the streets. Unrepentant Stalinist though he was, he always identified with the working class and its struggles.

In this ability to identify with his fellow workers, Gallacher was unlike another flawed and unrepentant Stalinist who worked in Scotstoun in the Second World War, Hugh MacDiarmid. Gallacher mentions Meechan's in his account of the 1915 strike given above. This was an ironworks that lay beside Albion and Yarrows and was founded about the same time. MacDiarmid, too old to fight, was conscripted into industrial work during the Second World War, and the three years he worked at Mechan's formed one of several periods he spent in Glasgow. MacDiarmid is one of Scotland's greatest 20th-century poets, possibly the greatest ever, and the only Scot who should have been awarded the Nobel Prize for Literature, in my opinion. But he was not a very likeable man.

Unlike people such as Gallacher, who became socialists because of their sympathy with what they felt capitalism had done to people, MacDiarmid – or Christopher Murray Grieve, as he was born – became a communist through contempt. Glasgow influenced many of his poems, especially his Hymns to Lenin, and in these there are lines of majestic outrage. From the 'Second Hymn':

Oh, it's nonsense, nonsense, nonsense,
Nonsense at this time o day
That breid-and-butter problems
S'ud be in ony man's way.

Sport, love, and parentage,
Trade, politics and law,
S'ud be nae mair tae us than braith
We hardly ken we draw.
Freein oor pooers for greater things
And fegs there's plenty o them
Though us that's trammelt in below
Cannae be tenty o them.

At the same time, he took refuge in a Nietzschean disdain for ordinary people, seeing the salvation of humanity lying in its imitating his own heroic self. He wrote, appallingly, in 'A Drunk Man Looks at the Thistle' that:

Millions o wimmin bring forth in pain
Millions o bairns that are no worth ha'en.

With his inability to relate to ordinary working men, MacDiarmid's time in Mechan's was torture. He took his breaks and meals alone, and was useless at his work, almost slicing his foot off through carelessness. It is unsurprising that he could not communicate with his fellow workers. In the 'Third Hymn to Lenin,' he talks of 'Glasgow's hordes' 'all bogged down in words that communicate no thought only mumbo jumbo, fraudulent crap, ballyhoo...'

Passing further along the cycle track, the Yarrows shipyard is next to the Albion. Still employing 2,000 workers, this must be the largest industrial unit in Glasgow – or even the whole of Clydeside – today. It largely survived because of the Cold War, since Yarrows was always a warship builder. The workers here brought honour to themselves in 1973, when they refused to finish work on a frigate bound for the Pinochet regime, which had overthrown Allende's reformist Government in Chile through a military coup. To the right of the cycle track here lie some curious cottages. Amidst the ubiquitous tenements of Dumbarton Road, these flat-roofed, brick-built buildings are eye-catching. They are known as the Yarrows Cottages, and were built for some of the many English workers who followed the shipyard from the Thames to the Clyde a century ago. On this occasion, local folklore is correct. I often think the majority of the population of Glasgow about 1900 must have been first-generation incomers of one sort or another. These Yarrows cottages are kept in much better repair than the Harland Cottages mentioned earlier, which are pretty fly-blown in appearance.

The track then crosses Dumbarton Road by the old railway bridge, which forms the internal boundary of Yokerstoun, and we have Scotstoun to the right and Yoker to the left, with something to see each way. On the right around Anniesland Road are found some of what must be the best council houses Glasgow Corporation ever built, a group of sparkling Art Deco detached blocks, with balconies and steel railings. Naturally, these were bought when tenants were allowed to purchase their properties and now change hands for many times the original price. The other council and housing association properties in Scotstoun are not so grand, though it is a well-kept and pleasant area. Nevertheless, in the past few years a food bank has been established here, an indication of the wealth polarisation that has taken place in areas like this.

Yoker, which takes us to – and beyond – the city boundary is on our left and the cycle track runs behind Dumbarton Road, following the former railway line's route back down towards the River Clyde, after passing under Kelso Street. Around here are plenty of dookits, and the ungainfully employed men who tend them. In fact, there would appear to be the highest concentration of dookits in the city in the back streets of Yoker. I was pleased to find a pal I had made on previous visits still there tending his deluxe dookit, which is surrounded by a tidy fenced garden area with a shed. Billy lamented the fact that the hobby was actually in decline and that when a lad, there were dookits on every corner and plot of waste ground in Yoker, though he agreed that they were conspicuous by their absence in nearby Scotstoun.

Half of Yoker is in Clydebank, on the west side of the Yoker Burn, the rest being in Glasgow. There was almost nothing at Yoker before the late-19th century, apart from Thomas Harvey's distillery, and Colin Robb's Inn, which lay on the east side of the burn and was largely used by drovers. The west side of the burn in Clydebank saw the coming of shipbuilding in 1877, but the east side waited till later for industrial development, when some exotic factories came to Yoker. In 1901, John Bull started manufacturing ships' propellers at Bull's Metal and Marine. Despite his very English name, Bull (probably Bulle) was a Norwegian entrepreneur. These works lay just east of the Yoker ferry, and is today part derelict, part covered in housing, and part occupied by a couple of small engineering works.

Another Scandinavian seeking to take advantage of Glasgow's

booming economy set up Halley Motors in Yoker, where he manufactured the famous Halley fire engines. Halley was a Dane, and his
works were later taken over by Albion Motors. These works are now
gone, and so too, probably to the greater relief of Yoker folk, are
White's chemical works. These were established beside the Forth and
Clyde Canal in north Yoker. We will later come across White, Lord
Overtoun, in relation to his chemical works at Shawfield in Rutherglen. The country's leading chrome manufacturer was also for a while
its leading iodine manufacturer, and produced this valuable commodity from Highland kelp at Yoker. Though not as polluting as his Rutherglen works, White's Yoker works were no model factory either, as
the workers dealt with caustic soda, bleaching soda and lime in dangerous concentrations. The coming of all these works a century ago
filled up the land between Clydebank and Glasgow with tenements,
and streets like Bulldale Street and Halley Street, whose names today
commemorate yesterday's lost employment.

At the end of a working day at Clydebank, if I didn't fancy a
two-way cycle, I'd leave the bike at work and take the bus home from
college, and this went straight through Yokerstoun, allowing a survey
of the Dumbarton Road, consisting mostly of decent Victorian four
storey tenements and their Glasgow Corporation three story sandstone slum clearance versions of tenement architecture from the early
20th century. At the far end of Yokerstoun, before Dumbarton Road
enters Whiteinch, lies a substantial middle-class housing development
of villas and terraces, which is now a conservation area. Even in this
city with an edge, there are few places where a street provides such a
stark social divide as Dumbarton Road does here. When the houses
were advertised in 1905 in the *Glasgow Herald*, prospective occupants
of properties in Danes Drive, Norse Road and the other streets were
reassured that the busy Dumbarton Road divided 'the classes from
the masses' at the southern side. And it still does, increasingly so, as
you approach the Scotstoun Showground to the north, whose sports
facilities were upgraded for the 2014 Commonwealth Games.

Yoker and Scotstoun have not changed a lot since the start of the
millennium, either socially or in terms of the built environment, but
it does still offer the occasional surprise. A walk along South Street
is an edgy experience, passing the former huge industrial concerns
now housing scrap merchants, car washes, cash and carry outlets
and similar enterprises. But just before Balmoral Street, in the former
Harland Building, is La Bodega, the best Spanish tapas bar in the city,

owned by a genuine Spaniard, whose main activity is running tango, salsa and flamenco dancing classes in the Dance with Attitude Studios, which feature live concerts as well as the restaurant. It's rough and ready and fun, and as funky as it gets in Yokerstoun.

CHAPTER SEVEN

Partick: Glasgow's Girnal No More

SUCH HAS BEEN the decline of Scots as the everyday language of Glasgow that not many people living there today would know what a girnal was. The cosmopolitan nature of the city has produced its own argot, which is very expressive and creative, but it contains relatively few Scots words. I was surprised on coming here from Aberdeen to find that people didn't know what a brander was, or a scaffie. A century ago, most Glasgow folk would still have known that a girnal was a grain chest and that Partick was the area where most of the city's grain was landed and processed.

Partick's eastern border with the city was the River Kelvin, which falls steeply to the Clyde in its latter stages, and which powered the early granaries along its banks. And here survived, till recently, the city's last grain mill. This was the Scotstoun Mill, owned by Rank Hovis, and it produced flour for their Duke Street bakery. Its closure in 2012 ended almost half a millennium of milling on the Kelvin. Timothy Pont's map of Lennox c.1600 shows a cluster of mills on the lower river, including the Bishop's Mill and a meal mill leased by the city of Glasgow. The incorporation of Glasgow bakers also owned two mills on the river, one called the Bunhouse Mill. Although other works, such as spinning and (timber) slit mills, used the water power of the Kelvin, it was grain mills that predominated. Upriver, behind the present day Kelvingrove Art Gallery, was the Clayslaps Mill, whose weir and lade with sluices are still visible.

Large-scale industrial flour milling began with the opening of the Scotstoun Mills in the 1840s, though as the Kelvin provided such cheap and efficient power, these were still water-operated, and remained so till the later expansion in the 19th century, when steam was applied. The Regent Flour mills were built across the Kelvin from the Scotstoun mill in the 1890s. Owned by the SCWS from 1903, this mill made the famous Lofty Peak flour (the site is now a car park for the Kelvin Hall). This cluster of mills large and small made it logical

Partick

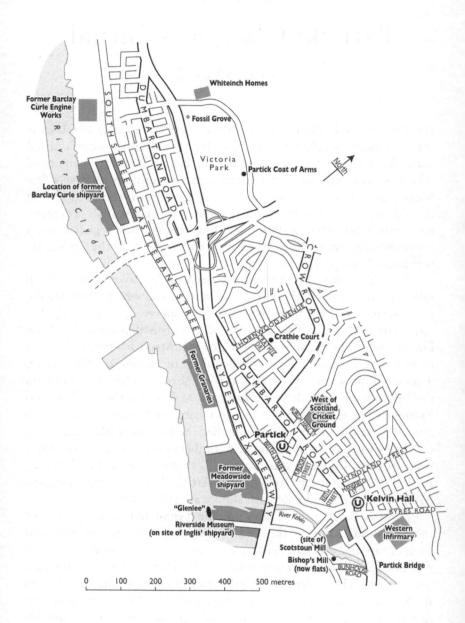

Partick Route Summaries

Route 1

1 Take the subway to Kelvinhall.
2 Cross Dumbarton Road and go down Cooperswell Street.
3 Cross the River Kelvin at Benalder Street (site of Bishop's Mill).
4 Head back up Bunhouse Road and across Argyle Street, working round behind the Kelvingrove Art Gallery and then up Kelvin Way.
5 Enter Kelvingrove Park and work back behind the University (Sunlight Cottages) to Dumbarton Road.
6 Go down Beith Street, past Purdon Street (Quaker Graveyard), and along to Hayburn Street and back again to Dumbarton Road.
7 Take Peel Street past the West of Scotland Cricket Ground.
8 Climb Tod's Brae to Partickhill Road.
9 Come back down Gardner Street (the view!) to Dumbarton Road, then proceed on past the library and Mansfield Park to the subway at Kelvinhall.

Approximate route time: 2.5 hours

Route 2 – Partick Improper

1 Take the subway or train to Partick.
2 Cross over the Clydeside Expressway using one of the bridges.
3 Walk along Castlebank Street, past the new riverside flats at Meadowside.
4 Continue west along South Street, where at Edzell Street you can gain the cycle track and get a good view of Barclay Curle's former engine works and its crane.
5 At Scotstoun Street, exit the track and work your way back to Dumbarton Road.
6 Cross Victoria Park Drive South to Westland Drive and the Fossil Grove in Victoria Park.
7 Return to Dumbarton Road and work your way east until you come to the Thornwood roundabout. (Be careful here as it can be treacherous!)
8 Head uphill at Thornwood Avenue, then along Crathie Drive (Crathie Court).
9 Trend generally south-east back to Dumbarton Road, and to the subway at Partick, where a wide choice of refreshment halts await.

Approximate route time: 3 hours

for the Clyde Navigation Trust to establish its grain depot at Mead-owside in Partick in the early 1900s, and until very recently the origin of most material for Glasgow's once ubiquitous *jeely peece* was in the girnals of Partick.

A good place to start an exploration of the area is at the bridge over the Kelvin, built to join Partick with Glasgow in 1877, just west of the Kelvin Hall. One end of the bridge bears the Glasgow coat of arms, the other that of Partick – which appropriately has millstones and a wheat sheaf on its crest. These crests are found on the cast iron supports of the south side of the bridge. The previous bridge, called the Snow Bridge, lies just to the north and is still open to pedestrians. From here a walk down Bunhouse Road and rightwards along Old Dumbarton Road brings you to the Wheatsheaf Buildings. Now flats, this cameo was built in the 1830s on the site of the original Bishop's Mill, and has delightful wheatsheaf motifs carved on its gables. It operated as a mill till the 1960s, and was water-driven till the 1950s.

No such new use was found for the derelict Partick Central station further on, and it was quietly demolished in the night. The land released by demolishing part of the Scotstoun Flour mills, however, is now occupied by stunning modern flats and all around here blocks of student accommodation are rising like mushrooms. Partick is being squeezed between old and new middle-class residential areas, between the West End and the new blocks of luxury apartments by the riverside where once stood the grain stores. An extensive, long-vacant cleared site to the west of the former Partick Central station has become the location of yet another block of student residences.

6.

This was formerly the Partick Foundry, and after closure in the '60s it became the site of unsightly scrap metal depots. However, back around 1600 this was the site chosen for the building of Partick Castle, a fortified house serving as the country home of George Hutcheson, co-founder of Glasgow Hutcheson's Hospital. Partick Castle was demolished in 1836.

Given its location (West

Regent's Mill circa 1900: One of the many mills on the Kelvin at Partick, this one was later owned by the SCWS. Older readers may remember its image on bags of flour – if their mothers shopped at the Co-op, that is.

End, University, Kelvingrove Museum etc.) and facilities (subway, railway, expressway) Partick has become a classic example of the benefits – or drawbacks, depending on your view – of the process of gentrification, with rising property values and rents leading to social cleansing in certain areas, and former working-class streets such as White Street becoming now predominantly middle class. As land values increase, it becomes more profitable to sell up than to produce, as the Scotstoun mill example proves. And by the Wheatsheaf buildings a small engineering works sold out to make way for a block of student flats. Gentrification promotes de-industrialisation, as well as resulting from it.

Before heading along Beith Street, it is worth visiting Glasgow's smallest graveyard. In amongst some modern housing on Keith Street lies the Quaker burial ground. Surrounded with metal railings, it has no gravestones, but simply a wooden plaque stating its function:

> Society of Friends Burial Ground
> Gifted by
> John Purdon 1711
> Last used 11-11-1857

The Quakers gifted the land to Partick, and a part of it was used for road building – in return for the site being kept in good order (which it appears to be) – and for 1s a year being donated to the Society of Friends. Does the Kooncil still pay the 5p? Apparently Purdon's wife was the first interred in the cemetery, and the family, which was a prominent one in 18th-century Partick and provided one of its early Provosts, is commemorated in neighbouring Purdon Street.

This area is the heart of the old pre-industrial village of Partick, and Keith Street used to be known as the Goat. The 'goat' in question was not four-footed, but an old Scots name for a small burn, one of which ran here. At the north end of the Goat was the Heid o' the Goat, a place where acrobats, quack doctors and religious and political agitators held court. A 19th-century Partick poet, Tom Burns, describes the scene in the broad Scots still spoken by the Glasgow working class at that period:

> Though its richt name's in print on a prominent spot
> The ane its best kent by is the heid o the Goat
> There tradesmen o every class you will find
> In guid Doric language expressing their mind

The old cottage buildings here were only demolished in the 1930s, and the Heid o' the Goat is now, with the demolition of a Comet store – now redeveloped as student flats.

Along Beith Street, past the rear entrance to Partick Subway, are some renovated sandstone tenements, but the most interesting building is the former Partick Fire Station, dating from 1906. This, too, has been converted to housing though the brick fire tower has been retained as a feature. The building itself is mostly brick-built, unusual for Glasgow before 1914, and also done in an almost Germanic style of architecture: Potsdam rather than Partick. Just beside the fire station at Meadow Road, access is gained to the Clydeside cycle track, which provides a high and traffic-free vantage point for further sightseeing.

The riverside here is now the site of a multi-million pound redevelopment, dominated by new housing in the high-rise model, once deemed suitable for the 'masses' but now more favoured, ironically, by the 'classes.' Though still uncompleted because of the economic crisis that erupted in 2008, this development is envisaged to extend from the Kelvin to the Clyde Tunnel. Much of the development is taking place on land once occupied by the huge red brick Meadowside Granary of the Clyde Navigation Trust. The 13-storey building was built by the Clyde Navigation Trust in 1911–13, at a cost of £130,000. Partick Thistle's move to Firhill in 1909, after over 30 years in Partick, was occasioned by the purchase of their stadium for construction of the granaries. In 1937 another granary, equally large, was built adjacent to the original one, and this Meadowside girnal of Glasgow could claim for a while to be one of the world's largest brick buildings. It gave a curiously reassuring feeling to see its bulk, and many people united in opposition to its destruction, arguing that the granary itself could have been converted to housing. Though the developers successfully argued against this, a significant part of the original construction materials were recycled into the new buildings. Whether their new residents will consider themselves recycled Partickonians, or commuters living in a riverside enclave, remains to be seen.

Partick was never the shipbuilding centre that Govan was, but it did have some important yards. From the cycle track, looking back towards the Kelvin's mouth, can still be seen the derelict brick and sandstone offices of the Meadowside Shipbuilding Yard, with its central tower in a sort of French Renaissance style. Hopefully this listed building will survive redevelopment in some form. One of the early owners of this yard, David Tod, became the first provost of

Partick. The second provost was John White, owner of the Scotstoun Mills, showing the tendency in the 19th century for local capitalists to exercise almost feudal (that is, uniting the political and the economic) powers in their locales, as provosts, MPs, JPs and the like. Tod and Macgregor's Pointhouse yard has the rather shameful honour of having made large amounts of money by constructing blockade-running ships for the slave-owning Confederacy during the American Civil War. The yard is the setting for a novel *The Blockade Runners* by Jules Verne, which also features Tod's house and other local landmarks.

Across the Kelvin mouth, and thus strictly speaking in Anderston, lay Inglis's Pointhouse yard, which specialised in paddle steamers, building the current *Waverley* in 1947, and the one of the same name which it replaced, and which was sunk at Dunkirk in 1940. The *Maid of the Loch*, currently being refurbished as an attraction at the Loch Lomond National Park, was built by Inglis's in 1952, but the yard closed ten years later, ending shipbuilding on the Kelvin. Inglis's yard had a famous set of sheer legs, 96 feet high, that stood till 1965. Now it has the even more impressive Riverside Museum on its former site, dedicated to the history of the transport industries of Glasgow and housed in the stunning architectural creation of Zaha Hadid – it was winner of the European Museum of the Year Award in 2013. But this should have been in Govan – both because of that area's stronger ship-building tradition, and because impoverished Govan needed it more than relatively prosperous Partick.

The construction of the Clydeside Expressway, built in part on what were considered slum properties that were then demolished, separated Partick from the River Clyde, and it also cut Partick itself asunder. At the Thornwood Roundabout, Dumbarton Road disappears under the Expressway in a maze of flyovers to re-emerge in the interesting district of Whiteinch. Few people consider it so today, but from its foundation, Whiteinch was part of the Partick burgh. Very little was found hereabouts till the Barclay Curle shipyard opened in the 1870s, moving from Anderston to a site just downriver from the Thornwood roundabout, a site now occupied by a variety of storage and small industrial usages. Starting with clippers and ending with liners, and building almost everything else in between, Barclay Curle was one of Glasgow's finest shipyards, a specialist builder that even managed to operate fully during the 1930s Depression. The yard has been demolished, but the marine engine works Barclay Curle built further downriver just before the First World War remain, with their fine hammerhead crane and the (listed) mansard roof enlivening the skyline, and the building is still in industrial use.

Whiteinch at one time was almost a model village. South of Dumbarton Road were the tenements for the workers in the shipyard, and to the north were rows of modest villas, Gordon Park, built in the 1880s for workers from the Scotstoun estate. These villas, clustered round the bowling green, now form a conservation area. Though not sharing in the gentrification going on in some areas of Partick, Whiteinch still has a reasonably coherent feel about it. It retains a primary school, though no secondary, and a local library; sadly the former Burgh Hall is a boarded up ruin. Some fine new social housing has been built towards the river in Edzell Street, amongst the grimmer council slum clearance projects of the 1930s. In Medwyn Street the splendid former Corporation Baths, built in the 1920 fashionable 'Wrenaissance' style, with the city's coat of arms boldly on the front-age, has been converted to flats, and on Dumbarton Road, at the corner of Hamlyn Street, is the excellent Cabin Restaurant. This claims to have been there since 1890, though hardly in its current Art Deco format. Sadly, Wilma, who used to provide impromptu Saturday night entertainment, has recently retired, but the place still has live music on occasions.

Cut off from Partick by the expressway, Whiteinch is now also cut off from Victoria Park to the north by the same road, which took over a slice of the park itself. A stroll through the park will not only bring you back to Partick proper, but also allow you to see the world-famous Fossil Grove, which it contains. Not just one, but a whole stand of fossilised scale trees, over 250 million years old, with their trunk-like roots, excellently preserved. Again, though not generally thought of as Partick today, Victoria Park was actually laid out by the burgh, and the burgh coat of arms, complete with Vikki's head, can be seen on one of its northern gateway entrances.

Two very interesting buildings are here, by the park on Westland Drive. Westercraigs was built as an orphanage in 1890, and is a grand sandstone villa now occupied by the Church of Scotland. Next to it is the Whiteinch Homes building, constructed as a poorhouse in 1890 but, unusually for Scotland, in the style of a medieval English alms-house, round a central courtyard. This building lay vacant for many years, but has been restored as Bield sheltered housing.

Renegotiating the over- and underpasses of the expressway brings you to the bottom of Thornwood Drive, cursing the negative effects such roads have on urban communities – and on urban pedestrianism. Thornwood has always had the reputation of being the posh part of Partick. Fine red sandstone tenements, well maintained and inhabited by the prosperous and respectable working and lower-middle classes stand here. There can be monotony in respectability, but in Thornwood this is broken by some of the best council housing in the city. There are several blocks of good municipal housing, and at Crathie Drive is a building of exceptional merit and interest that dominates the Thornwood skyline. This is Crathie Court, built in 1952, but its Art Deco features show pre-war design influence in the projecting balconies and lines of porthole windows. Set in well-maintained grounds, the building was designed as 88 flats for single people at a time when almost all housing was for the standard nuclear family. In recognition of its importance, the building gained a Saltire Award. Crow Road takes us back down to Dumbarton Road, and slightly scruffier East Partick. But even here the relentless march of gentrification continues. Up Norval Street, off Crow Road, generations of 'Pertick wummen' toiled in Tomlinson's factory making cardboard boxes; you could watch them from the passing blue trains at Partick station. Today, its bright pastel exterior and atrium roof proclaim it as The Printworks apartment block.

Moving along Dumbarton Road is a pleasant pedestrian experience, as the line of the street is virtually unbroken and the commercial premises are all occupied and well maintained, in contrast to those in rather more run-down Whiteinch. It was not always so pleasant however, and in 1875 a procession of Irish nationalists on Dumbarton Road was attacked by political opponents, leading to three days of rioting. This was ended only when special constables were sworn in to support the police in quelling the disturbances. Partick's other great unrest was the Rent Strikes of 1915, when the area was one of the strongest in the city for action against profiteering. These struggles were led by the Partick housewives, harassing the landlords' agents with pails of refuse and laying about them with pots and pans. The women in turn were led by ILP member Helen Crawfurd. The women of Partick appear a fierce brood. A famous 19th-century Partick lass was Big Rachael, all six foot four inches and 16 stones of her. She worked as a labourer in the Meadowside shipyard and later as a foreman (-person?) in a brickworks. In the riots of 1875, she was enrolled as a special constable.

Before 1914, Partick was a stronghold of Orangeism, especially in

its shipyards, where many had come to work from Ulster. It is not generally recognised that 40 per cent of the city's Irish immigration came
from Ulster (though, of course, many of these were Catholics, like those
from the rest of Ireland) – and this was largely responsible for bringing
the poison of sectarianism to Glasgow. John Paton, in his *Proletarian
Pilgrimage*, writes of his dismay at finding such a phenomenon in
Glasgow, so absent in his native Aberdeen. Paton's book was published
in the 1930s, and he describes how before the First World War, an ILP
propaganda lorry was set ablaze by Orangemen in Partick, and the
comrades decided to assert their right of free speech by a march along
Dumbarton Road. They were ambushed by well-organised groups
emerging from closes to attack the procession. Paton comments:

> We'd no chance at all against them. They were tough fellows
> from the shipyards who enjoyed nothing so much as a good fight.
> It wasn't a defeat, it was a rout.

However, even before the war, these diehard Tory Orangemen were
prepared to listen to socialist speakers, rather than simply attack them.
Paton recounts the factory gate meeting at a Whiteinch shipyard
(probably Barclay Curle's), addressed by his fellow Aberdonian, Jamie
Kessack, who immediately grasped their attention with his opening
words:

> Last Sunday I stood on the Custom House steps at Belfast, girdled
> by the steel of the bayonets of the circle of soldiers who enclosed
> me...

Kessack got a 'rapt audience and hearty applause at the end'. The war
and its aftermath seriously weakened, though did not kill, political
Orangeism, in Partick as elsewhere.

A wee trip off Dumbarton Road to Burgh Hall Street allows us to
take a look at the centre of Partick government from 1852 till 1912.
In that latter year an Act of Parliament overturned Partick's wishes to
remain independent and a piper played 'Lochaber No More'. Would
that, a century on, our politicians had the courage to similarly add
Glasgow's present periphery to the city. But Partick, Govan and Maryhill were working-class areas; Bearsden and Newton Mearns are not.

Partick Burgh Halls, though well used and under renovation,
cannot compete with those of Maryhill and Govan, either in exterior
embellishment or interior furnishings. But it certainly has a better view,
looking out as it does across the lawns of the West of Scotland Cricket

ground to the villas of Partickhill rising beyond. Once a curling pond and bowling green, the site has a place in football history, in that it hosted the first Scotland–England international in 1872. Not only roads and railways can separate social classes, so too can parks, or sports fields, and while at the north end of the cricket ground you are in patrician Partickhill, on the south you are in proletarian Partick. Partick Library, which is passed on Dumbarton Road on the right heading back to the Cross, used to have a nice wee exhibition on the history of the area, though it was missing on my last visit.

Between Hyndland Street and Mansfield Street is one of the few cleared areas on Dumbarton Road, where a block of tenements was demolished to make way for a recreation area, since known as Mansfield Park, which hosts events like farmers' markets and has a sports area laid out in it. On Mansfield Street are found the offices of *An Commun Ghaidhlig* (dedicated to promoting Gaelic and language) and a Gaelic bookshop, occupying the ground floor of a solid set of tenements, built, as it proudly states, by the St George's Co-operative Society. It is appropriate that this shop is located here, as Partick has always had a tradition of Gaelic immigrants and Gaelic churches. It is estimated that in Partick and the wider West End of Glasgow there is a greater concentration of Gaelic speakers than anywhere outside Lewis in the Western Isles.

Though this tradition was swelled by the influx of Gaels to work on various jobs on the Clyde, it goes further back to when Partick was on the drove route into Glasgow from the West Highlands. The drovers came down what is now Crow Road (Crow is from the Gaelic *croadh*, cattle) and overnighted in Partick before moving into Glasgow. A famous inn, Granny Gibbs's, was the destination of these drovers, and lay near the present Thornwood roundabout. This inn was built by Granny Gibbs's husband in 1796 when droving was at its height, and demolished a century later, when it had ended. Drovers kept their sheep and cattle in her pens, before moving into Glasgow. Her thatched dwelling was commemorated by another of the prolific Partick poets, George Boyce:

> The drovers passing east and west
> Knew her wee hoose of call
> With Highland whisky o the best
> She would supply them all.

This tradition of Highland hostelry continues in the pub on the corner of Mansfield Street, the Lismore, which does much to support Gaelic music and culture. The owners have also commissioned a set of fine stained glass windows in the pub, commemorating the Highland Clearances, and showing Highlanders at work. These panels have clearly been influenced by those of Stephen Adam in Maryhill Burgh Halls (see Chapter Nine: Maryhill Unlocked). Partick's taverns have a long tradition of conviviality. Bunhouse Road is not named after a bakery but after an inn called the Bun and Yill Hoose, which formerly stood there. In Strang's *Glasgow and its Clubs* we read of the Partick Duck Club, which flourished in the early 19th century. This group of Glasgow worthies were mainly from the Trades House, and used to repair to Partick to feast at the Bun Hoose on roast duck and peas, washed down with punch. One of their number was immortalised in the couplet:

> The ducks of Partick quacked for fear
> Crying 'Lord preserve us, there's MacTear!

The profusion of fat ducks in Partick was due to their feasting on the products and by-products of the grain mills on the Kelvin. The old Bun Hoose apparently had a lintel dated 1695 over the door, but was demolished in 1849.

Back at the foot of Byres Road we are at Partick Cross. Here is a curious scene. On the one hand, good quality red sandstone tenements, and on the other, every inch of vacant land is filled with lofts and apartments. On the one hand the spread of upmarket restaurants and cafés, on the other the survival of little works, almost sweatshops – and probably the greatest concentration of charity shops in Glasgow. Does this signify a hidden poverty in Partick, or just that the nearby denizens of the more prosperous West End areas can spot a bargain when they see one? Its worst housing long ago demolished by the construction of the Expressway, Partick does not give out the air of dereliction of some other inner-city working-class areas of Glasgow. The population of the ex-burgh, which grew from about 5,000 in 1852 to 56,000 in 1912, declined in the 20th century to about half that figure, but is steadily rising again.

The university was never in Partick. But the Western Infirmary, or rather the Anderson College of Medicine as it originally was, did lie within the burgh boundaries – but only just – after the institution was moved from Glasgow in 1889. A dramatic relief by Pittendrigh MacGillivray adorns the building, showing doctors performing an

Partick Rent Strike 1915: Partick and Govan were the two bastions of the strike against landlord profiteering in 1915, but the slogans on the posters show that the rent strike was in no way an anti-war movement.

operation. He was an Aberdeen artist who did much work in Glasgow, and whose sculptures of shipyard workers in Govan we have already noted. Just within Partick also, and bearing an address in Dumbarton Road, is the curious Tudor Cottage on the north bank of the Kelvin, within Kelvingrove Park. This was an exhibit of model workers' housing from Leverhulme's Port Sunlight factory on Merseyside. It was shown at the International Exhibition in Kelvingrove in 1901, and later donated to the city for use as a park keeper's dwelling. This is the last, or first, dwelling in Partick and a good place to end.

In 1912, they played 'Lochaber No More'; such is the rate of change in Partick, as it becomes swallowed up by the West End of Glasgow, that it may soon be 'Partick No More'. Close to the West End, to the university and the Art Gallery, Partick was always that bit different from other working-class areas in Glasgow, and it may soon be an area not only with little working-class employment, but with an ever-decreasing working-class population. The idea that things can be otherwise in a free market (let's just call it for what it is, i.e. capitalist) economy is an illusion. If areas decline, poor people move in, if areas go upmarket, rich people move in. That is what is happening in Partick more than anywhere else in the city.

CHAPTER EIGHT

Anderston:
Glasgow's Barometer

'GLASGOW MADE THE Clyde and the Clyde made Glasgow,' so the old saying goes.

From my window in St Vincent Crescent on the edge of the Anderston district, I watched for a quarter century as Glasgow remade its river in the hope that the new Clyde would help remake Glasgow. Initially I looked out to a River Clyde past its industrial greatness, but still alive. From the giant crane at Finnieston, boilers and desalination plants would be lifted onto ships to be exported over the globe. The trio of smaller cranes at the iron ore terminal across the Clyde still unloaded cargoes of iron ore for Ravenscraig and other steelworks. At New Year, there were enough ships docked on the river to play a symphony on their sirens to announce midnight. Now, there is only the *Waverley* paddle steamer.

A nightmare period ensued, as the cranes were blown up and the docks were filled in. The warehouses were demolished and splendid industrial architecture, such as the Italianate Pumping House at Queen's Dock, fell into decay. The Garden Festival in 1988 briefly gave a facelift to the riverside, but just as swiftly the cosmetic effect faded with little permanent left behind. Today it is different. While not everyone might approve of all that is happening on the banks of the Clyde, such as the new futuristic edifices appearing like mushrooms, there is more activity on the river, and more optimism for the future, than for decades.

I am a frequent walker by the river and it is easy to be nostalgic about its great industrial and seafaring past. On one walk I met an 80-year-old man from Kinning Park, who similarly walks the banks. He told me he had been a docker on the river all his life; when his docker father had lost his job in the 1930s, Wee Matt (he was tiny) admitted he stayed alive by stealing the cream off what he delivered as a milk boy. 'It's much better noo,' Matt was definite, 'The weans hae thae computers and things. They widnae want ma life.'

St Vincent Crescent Lane leads to Kelvinhaugh Street, and a short distance away behind Yorkhill Hospital lies the now closed Kelvin-haugh Primary School, built in Victoria's Jubilee in 1887, with a sculpture of Old Vic frowning down at you from the walls. Its original pupils looked down from their heights to the docks of the Second City of the Empire, which had been opened by Victoria herself in 1877, on the site of the demolished Stobcross Mansion House. The site of the former Queen's Dock can be reached from Kelvinhaugh Street by a footbridge over the Clydeside Expressway. Ignore the traffic noise and you can take in fine views of the river far downstream.

A good point from which to view the changing riverside is the walkway that passes the Crowne Plaza Hotel. No tradition here, but stark modernity in the phallic black glass hotel and at Norman Foster's SECC (nicknamed The Armadillo by the locals). This is Glasgow's copy of the Sydney Opera House (Glasgow is brash enough to copy anything; across the river is the Grand Ole Opry, an answer to Memphis's). Now we also have the new Hydro events space to contemplate. The site of the SECC saw Glasgow's biggest demonstration since the days of the UCS work-in in the early 1970s. In the spring of 2003, as he prepared to take us into the disaster of the Iraq war based on a mishmash of fabricated lies, Blair was due to address the Labour Party Conference at the SECC. Eighty thousand people turned up there in the afternoon to protest against the war, showing that Glasgow may have lost most of its industry, but it has not lost its radical traditions. Blair, however, cowardly sneaked by in the morning, did his speech, and made himself scarce.

But relics of the past mingle pleasingly with the present, in the black latticework of the Finnieston Crane, installed in here 1935. Last used in the early 1980s, 'the cran' is now a symbol of Glasgow (though, ironically, it was built by Cowans and Sheldon in Carlisle). The main function of the Finnieston Crane was to lift the locomotives, driven down the tramlines from Springburn, onto the waiting trans-port ships. Beneath the cran is the Hilton Garden Inn, a rather functional-looking new hotel, whose splendid food belies its image, and where a riverside terrace, the only one in Glasgow, allows a refreshment stop. The south side of the river is now being repopulated with imaginative pyramidal blocks of flats, next to ones of more con-ventional design, but painted a riot of pastel colours in an attempt to brighten up the grey Glasgow light. This has not met with universal approval, but I like it. The Millennium, aka Squinty, Bridge now links these two banks of the riverside.

Anderston

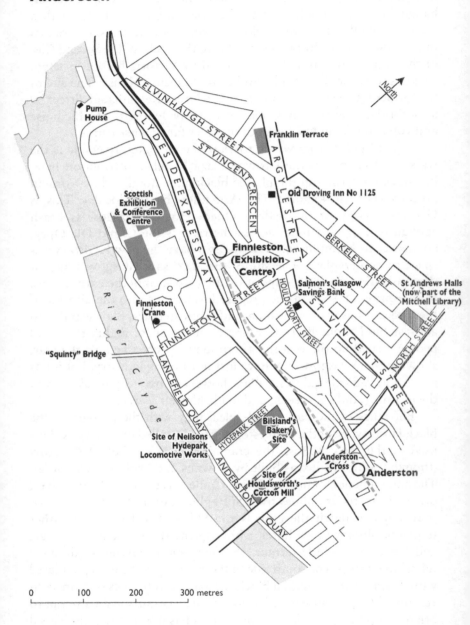

North

Pump House

KELVINHAUGH STREET

CLYDESIDE EXPRESSWAY

ST VINCENT CRESCENT

ARGYLE STREET

Franklin Terrace

Old Droving Inn No 1125

BERKELEY STREET

Scottish Exhibition & Conference Centre

Finnieston (Exhibition Centre)

FINNIESTON STREET

HOULDSWORTH STREET

Salmon's Glasgow Savings Bank

ST VINCENT STREET

St Andrews Halls (now part of the Mitchell Library)

Finnieston Crane

River Clyde

"Squinty" Bridge

LANCEFIELD QUAY

NORTH STREET

HYDEPARK STREET

Site of Neilsons Hydepark Locomotive Works

Bilsland's Bakery Site

ANDERSTON QUAY

Anderston Cross

Anderston

Site of Houldsworth's Cotton Mill

0   100   200   300 metres

Anderston Route Summary

1 Take a train to Anderston Cross.

2 Emerge in a world-class concrete planning blight horror and fight your way down to Anderston Quay.

3 Head westwards along Anderston Quay, then along Lancefield Quay to the Squinty Bridge (Clyde Arc) and the Finnieston Crane.

4 Continue along the Clyde, past the SECC, until the heliport is gained and then a footbridge crosses the Expressway to Kelvinhaugh Street.

5 Walk up to Argyle Street, taking a look around the corner at Franklin Terrace, then continue down this thoroughfare.

6 Take a possible diversion to St Vincent Crescent and consider refreshments at the Hidden Lane Tearoom, down a pend just after the Drovers Inn. Then proceed to Houldsworth Street, passing behind the Anderston Wall, and regaining Anderston Cross station.

7 Look at a picture of Anderston Cross pre-1970, and weep for what it has become!

Approximate route time: 2.5 hours

Both banks of the river here are being lined with new expensive apartment dwellings, many of innovative and striking design, or with former warehouses, converted to flats. Amongst all this is a fond relic of the past, the *Waverley*, and if it is in port, the world's last ocean-going paddle steamer, built in Glasgow in 1947, is a photo opportunity not to be missed. Its berth has been moved to the Science Centre from its former Kingston Bridge location. The bridge towered over the brick-and-tile palace of Snodgrass's Washington Grain Mills, a building that reminded us that this was granary country. It was a construction that seemed as if it should have been in the middle of the American Prairies or Chicago. Still miraculously in operation as a grain mill in the late 1990s, it was acquired for reconstruction but regrettably has been demolished to provide land for a new build which has not as yet occurred over a decade later.

Also demolished for a commercial expansion that failed to materialise was the former lodging house beside the Kingston Bridge. Anderston was always the centre of Glasgow's 'models,' having five out of the city's 19 such institutions before the First World War, even though Anderston had a mere five per cent of the city's population. Most of the people who used to work on the riverside hereabouts lived in the district of Anderston. From a single habitation in the middle of the 18th century, Anderston had achieved a population of over 30,000 to become one of the most crowded districts in Glasgow by 1900.

Originally called Stobcross, Anderston was planned as a weavers' village in the 1720s by one Anderson, owner of the Stobcross estate. A Weavers Society was formed in 1738. Anderston prospered and grew to a population of 4,000 in the 1790s when weaving fortunes were at their height. The women worked in the spinning industry and the first spinning mill was established about 1750 by Henry Menteith, who brought over 50 French female workers to teach the locals. Henry had fought against the Jacobites at Falkirk in 1746, and had previously had his cattle stolen for refusing to pay blackmail to Rob Roy (of whom more later).

Around 1800, Henry Houldsworth opened one of the first steam-powered cotton spinning factories in Scotland at Cheapside Street in Anderston. This was built without a piece of wood in it, to be fireproof. Houldsworth became Anderston's first Provost when it became a burgh in 1824, only for it to be annexed (with his full approval) by Glasgow in 1846. Hard times in the 1830s caused Houldsworth and other employers to cut wages and the Association of Operative Cotton Spinners called a strike in 1837. One nab (or scab) was shot and killed, and in a show-trial five of the leaders of the union were charged with murder, acquitted but convicted of a lesser charge and sentenced to seven years transportation, later commuted to various terms of imprisonment. Meanwhile the witnesses shared a £500 reward from the employers and emigrated. The strike and the repression crippled the union. On a lighter note, this period of textile dominance produced the famous song 'The Bleacher Lass o' Kelvinhaugh,' whose heroine worked in the Anderston mills:

> Says I 'My lassie where are you going?
> What do you do by the Broomielaw?'
> Says she, 'Kind sir I'm a bleacher lassie
> In Cochrane's Bleachfields in Kelvinhaugh.'

As elsewhere in Glasgow, textiles gave way to heavy engineering, and just as it has a claim to be one of the birthplaces of Glasgow's textile industry, so Anderston can claim to be one of the birthplaces of many

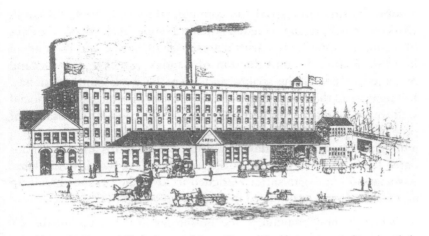

Houldsworth's Cotton Mill: An image of the mill once it had been converted to a bonded warehouse gives an idea of its size. This switch from manufacturing to service industries happened earlier in Anderston than elsewhere.

of its heavy industries. The first shipyard on the Upper Clyde was the Stobcross yard of Barclay and Curle, which opened in 1818 before moving in 1870 to Whiteinch. William Simpson ('Crimea' Simpson, so-called because he was the official war artist in that conflict) was born in Anderston and painted an interesting picture of a launch at this yard, published in his *Glasgow in the Forties*. Neilson's locomotive works were set up in Hydepark Street to be near the river, but moved to Springburn (though retaining the Hydepark works name) in 1876. Similarly William Macfarlane's Saracen Foundry moved to Anderston in the 1860s from the East End, but then moved to a greenfield site in Possil. The problem for all these large-scale enterprises was lack of space to expand in the crowded riverside district, and as they grew, they moved out. Thus Anderston was again a pointer towards Glasgow's industrial future, in that well before 1914 the area was moving towards dependence on the service and unskilled industries, towards de-skilling and de-industrialisation.

By 1914 the area's employment was dominated by casual and unskilled labour for men in the docks and warehouses, and by industrial employment such as textiles and bakeries. Bilsland's Bakery was opened here as Bilsland Bros. in the 1880s by William Bilsland, who soon afterwards became Provost of Glasgow. Its red brick construction, with the firm's name visible, still dominates the skyline view to the river, but the bakery is long closed and the building is now honeycombed by small industrial and commercial units. In 1884 Bilsland's workers struck, trying to reduce their 72-hour week (that's six days of 12-hour shifts for the arithmetically challenged), and then again in 1889 against the introduction of Sunday working, but Bilsland managed to defeat the strikes and keep the trades unions at bay, feeling instead the 39s (less than £2) a head per annum spend on social welfare for his workers was enough. In 1922, along with thousands of other bakery workers, Bilsland's 500-strong workforce went on strike, aiming for an eight-hour day. The firm called in scabs and accommodated them in the Hydepark works, and the Glasgow Master Bakers' Association (an organisation designed to keep the price of bread up and wages down) announced in the *Glasgow Herald* that:

> Some of the Communists and Bolsheviks in the ranks (of the workers) have been spoiling for a fight, and they won't be happy till they have got one.

The strike was lost and the workers had to continue clocking on at 2.30am for the night shift, and unskilled female labour, cheaper than employing time-served men, was introduced into the increasingly mechanised bakeries.

In 1907, the same *Glasgow Herald* cited above had characterised

The 1837 Spinners' Strike: Thomas Hunter, Peter Hacket, Richard McNeil, James Gibb and William McLean, executive committee members of the Glasgow Cotton Spinners' Association, each subject to seven years' transportation on the evidence of bribed witnesses.

Anderston as a district where men could be found 'loitering in a stag-
nant pool about certain large centres of employment and doing an odd
day's work now and again'. As it became impoverished, Anderston
became increasingly overcrowded as people sought to pay lower rents.
Much of the housing in Anderston was not of the best quality anyway,
and looking in David Glenday's pamphlet *Old Anderston* at photographs of its grim and blackened streets provokes little nostalgia. The
main thoroughfares like Argyle Street and Stobcross Street were quite
reasonable, but the narrow streets linking these and St Vincent Street
contained some of the city's worst housing. Though some of this was
demolished in the 1930s, by 1951 Anderston still had 50 per cent of
its people living without an inside toilet and a population density of
1.5 to a room – and in the bad bits it was worse.

This is not to say Anderston was all slum: there was a better part
which lay to the north of St Vincent Street, toward the Mitchell Library
and the St Andrews Halls. Here lived many who worked in the Wylie
and Lochead Cabinetmakers' works; good, steady, well-paid work.
This works has now been converted into the block of flats south of
the Mitchell Library. 'The Mitchell' is well known as Europe's largest
public reference library, but the St Andrew's Hall was destroyed by a
fire in the 1960s and rebuilt as a Mitchell extension. The Halls were
the scene of many political meetings, most especially the rowdy con-
frontation between the Clyde Workers' Committee and Lloyd George
in 1915 over the dilution crisis. The shop stewards of the engineering
works wanted wage rises and workers' control over the dilution of
labour, and had organised strikes to press their aims. John Maclean
argued that these demands were tantamount to workers' control over
the war effort, which war the CWC should instead have been opposing.
And he was right.

Anderston's reputation as one of Glasgow's poorest areas with
terrible housing meant that when Comprehensive Redevelopment
became the vogue in the 1960s, little of the area was destined to
remain standing. But much more was demolished than was necessary,
the reason being, quite simply, that the land was needed for the M8
motorway and the Kingston Bridge. When this opened in 1970, much
of Anderston simply vanished, including entire streets such as Stobcross Street. Anderston admittedly had not a vast amount worth
saving, but the demolition of Anderston Cross, with JJ Burnet's marvelous railway station building, built in 1896, was a planning atrocity.
Anderston Cross railway station is still there, approached by what

must be the most agoraphobic concrete litter-strewn space in the city. Anderston in fact lost two Crosses to redevelopment. Peden's Cross used to be at the corner of Argyle Street and Elderslie Steet, and was named after a building with a representation of the Covenanter prophet sculpted on it. Alexander Peden reputedly stood here some-time in the mid-17th century and prophesied that the site would become the centre, or the new Cross, of Glasgow. To some extent with the M8 nearby, it has become so.

Anderston once stretched to almost Central Station, but today it has shrunk. It is not only that the M8 and Kingston Bridge cuts it off from its former eastern territories, it is that these in turn have become the home of several chain hotels like the Marriot, of MOD offices and, down by the Broomielaw, the International Financial Services District with its array of shiny new office blocks. This is now City Centre, and no longer part of our Anderston remit. The recent conversion of the Road to Nowhere, a never completed M8 flyover, into a cycling and walking track may be fine for city centre cycling commuters, but will have hardly any effect on Anderston itself.

These redevelopments reduced the population of the rest of Ander-ston to about 10,000 by 1981, which was just about what it was when annexed by Glasgow in 1846, and a third of what it had been in 1951. In the last two decades, like some other inner-city working-class areas, the population has been rising again as new housing is constructed on brown sites or as former factories and warehouses are converted to flats. Pleasing Housing Association blocks in pastel shades with balconies were built in the 1990s on Argyle Street, one with a doorway commemorating the Anderston Weavers Society. These were mingled at first with the severer '60s architecture of square blocks of medium-rise houses, but recently almost all of these have been demolished and more attractive blocks, lining the street and restoring its linear pattern, have been built. The 'Anderston Wall' on St Vincent Street might seem to be an example of the worst of '60s architecture, but look closely and you will see not a broken window, no graffiti – and no litter. And that is true of Anderston in general; it is, for some reason, the least litter-strewn and graffiti-ridden inner-city area of Glasgow. The Anderston Wall flats were recently renovated when the residents overwhelmingly voted against their demolition.

At a detached bit of Argyle Street is a wonderful tenement building in Art Nouveau style, the Glasgow Savings Bank, with ornate metal work, fine sandstone sculptures and a marvelous coloured mosaic over the entrance doorway. The interior, if you can gain access, is equally grand and boasts a splendid fireplace in the Glasgow Style. Built by James Salmon II around 1900, the building has suffered some neglect and an unwelcome horrendous brick and concrete intrusion, but this still must be one of Glasgow's finest tenements. Another tenement block nearer the town centre houses Two Fat Ladies, formerly the Buttery, a famous Glasgow restaurant, in what was possibly, from the evidence of the symbols on it, housing built by the Freemasons Society. These two are the only tenements left in the heart of what was formerly Anderston's tenement core.

Further along Houldsworth Street, past the pyramidal Anderston Church of Scotland, an unsuccessful '60s attempt at modernity, and past the demolished the Salvation Army headquarters, lie some semi-derelict 19th-century warehouses and factory buildings, a brass foundry, an iron foundry and a saw and file works. These have ornate polychrome brickwork and fine arches windows, and are well worth restoring, for they give you an impression of what this area was like until 1950: a dense warren of small factories and tenements, now to be seen only in old photographs. Anderston's poverty was reflected in the fact that the first Salvation Army foundation in Scotland was opened here in 1879, a presence which continues today. Another first was the Lipton's store in Stobcross Street in 1871, which began the grocer's empire. The shop and the very street disappeared with the construction of the Clydeside Expressway.

It may seem strange that the heavily industrial area of Anderston, which was one of the poorest in Glasgow, lay cheek by jowl with one of the city's more prestigious middle-class developments. But from these derelict factory properties in Houldsworth Street can be seen the impressive wrought-iron ornamentation of a former Edwardian public toilet at the entrance to Minerva Street, which in turn leads to St Vincent Crescent. It was originally called Stobcross Crescent, but the residents thought St Vincent sounded more upmarket, and changed the name.

As Glasgow developed in the 19th century, and the centre and east became crowded and polluted, the middle classes moved west. On the Stobcross estate an extensive development of terraced flats was planned, with pleasure gardens, curling ponds and the like, subsequent to Anderston's incorporation into Glasgow in the 1840s. Minerva Street was built in 1849 in a rather Edinburgh style – with its top-curved ground-floor windows – and then work on the Crescent began, being finally finished in 1851. The architect of both was Alexander Kirkland, who himself lived in a flat in the Crescent. There was a problem of avoiding monotony in the longest crescent in Britain outside Royal Crescent in Bath. Kirkland did this through its serpentine form, by having pillared porticos at irregular intervals and by having a variety of sizes of living space internally. The house interiors featured marble fireplaces and elaborate cornicing, as well as other features. The houses were occupied by solid middle-class people, and many of them had indwelling servants. Rents were from £40 to £70 a year at a time when working-class rents averaged £5 a year. From their windows over the quarter-century following construction, they saw as much change as I myself did when I lived there, though possibly they viewed it with less enthusiasm.

As the industrialisation of Glasgow moved west, a large railway marshalling yard was built to the south of the Crescent, to give access to the Queen's Dock, and the planned larger prestige housing development dropped. By 1864, when Thomas Sulman went up in a balloon to draw his *View of Glasgow*, the Crescent is shown surrounded by industrial development, although the docks had not yet been built. The enclave rapidly became hemmed in by factories and tenement properties, and began a gradual decline. By the 1950s, the Crescent was blighted by business/office usage and by multiple occupancy. Ladies of commercial affection also used flats in the street, and it gained a reputation of having underworld connections. My own flat had been previously tenanted by travelling people, a room to a family. Upstairs was a Robin Hood-type amiable outlaw, who specialised in stripping the lead off neighbouring roofs, while across the landing from him an old lady, spinstered by the First World War, sat amongst her antiques and played the spinet as a reminder of the street's fashionable origins.

As late as 1970 plans were afoot to demolish the whole area (part of the flanking entrance to Minerva Street was actually demolished). However, times changed. People began to see the attractions of living off-city-centre, off-West-End, and moved in, after which a fight led to restoration in the 1980s, instead of demolition – and the granting of A-listed architectural status. One delight of the street is that it must have the highest concentration of bowling greens in the world; three line its southern side, on the site of the former curling pond. One of these greens presents a cameo in its gate, in the form of a fine example of Saracen Foundry cast iron from 1860, made when this works lay nearby in Anderston.

Because of its rollercoaster history, the Crescent is possibly the most socially mixed area in Glasgow. Many famous people live or have lived in the Crescent, including John Cairney, Jimmy MacGregor and Daniella Nardini: it attracts freelance artists, writers and the semi-bohemian alike. But the Crescent also has many working-class residents who moved in when it had lost its earlier middle-class status (our close had a BP oil executive and a North Sea roustabout living in it at the same time), and in the street there are sheltered housing and housing association properties. As a contrast to this, we also had a viscount (impoverished)! Living here was great fun, and provided a social education in one street for my son. All human life was – and is – definitely here!

Round the corner in Argyle Street it is – and was – a different world. Till about 2000 this was a decidedly working-class street, with the usual array of working-class shops, many admittedly not very good, and a large number of traditional working-class pubs. In the last 15 years or so, all this has changed and the Finnieston Strip, as it is monikered, though remaining working-class residentially, has become host to an amazing variety of upmarket restaurants, drinking places and shops, whose clients are the inhabitants of the West End proper and the student population which lives near the University, and not the local population, who are squeezed into the few remaining traditional pubs like The Grove and the local Tesco, whilst the passers through buy fish suppers in boutique fish and chip shops for £7.50 and £3 spelt and rye loaves at the local health food store. As the housing in this section of Argyle Street is of reasonable quality, one can see Finnieston as a suitable case for social cleansing.

A couple of buildings on this part of the street are worthy of notice. In the riot of inner-city wildlife of the human variety lies the Argyle Street Ash (or Elm – I leave it to arboriculturalists to decide), which now towers above the four-storey tenement building in whose front garden it is rooted – Glasgow's most famous tree. And unlike the one on the city's coat of arms, this one grew! The fine if slightly tatty block here is called Franklin Terrace and was built as middle-class residences in 1845 – way before the other tenements abouts, and to an exceptionally high quality, with very large rooms. It has the distinction of having provided the lodgings of the man Madeleine Smith is alleged to have poisoned in 1857, Pierre Emile L'Angelier. These again were middle-class dwellings. In *The Tenement* (1979), Frank Worsdall makes the point that almost any tenement still standing from pre-1880 was a middle-class one; the working-class tenements built before about 1890 were so poor that hardly any examples remain. The working-class tenements which do remain date from the replacement of blonde sandstone with the more durable red sandstone from about 1890 and the Glasgow Police Act of 1892, which stipulated that all such buildings had to be constructed with inside toilets and forbade the insertion in them of single-end dwellings.

Heading back down Argyle Street towards Anderston proper, you pass at No. 1125 the oldest remaining building in the district, a cottage-like structure. This was a former inn on the road from Glasgow to Partick, and probably dates from the early 18th century, or even earlier. The inn was at a drovers' stance, the last stop before the cattle markets of Glasgow. Rob Roy was said to use it in his droving days, for an overnight stop, and reputedly had his favourite drinking cup kept for his personal use. We have already seen previously how, when he stooped to less honourable pursuits such as blackmail, Rob fell out with Menteith of Anderston. In those days Stobcross Mansion stood where the SECC now is and between were fields where Anderstonians grazed their cattle. There are records of Menteith claiming that Rob grazed his own beasts here – and then departed in the morning with some of Menteith's added to the herd!

The inn ceased to trade in 1902 and became first a cabinetmakers works and latterly a glass-beveling workshop. It was used for the television production of Roddy Macmillan's play, *The Bevellers*, in the 1980s. MacMillan, celebrated for his TV roles in *Para Handy* and *Daniel Pyke*, was born in Cranston Street, Anderston, and worked for some time as a glass beveller, possibly in that very shop. In keeping with the social trend of the area, the former inn has now become a quality restaurant. A few doors further along is a pend, the entrance to a backcourt that used to host a variety of small workshops and tradesmen, some of whose faded adverts still mark the entrance. Now it is another addition to Glasgow's cultural scene, the Hidden Lane. There, as well as a wonderful award-winning tea shop which serves real High Teas, there are a variety of artists' studios, galleries and other artisanal creative enterprises. In Finnieston there is now no shortage of decent eateries and cultural attractions, but you would be hard put to get your glass beveled or your plumbing fixed.

In some ways Anderston has been a barometer of Glasgow's development. Starting as a textile centre, it moved into heavy engineering, and then into service and unskilled work, in each case in advance of the city's working-class districts as a whole. There is little doubt it fell far, and even less doubt that it deserved better from the planners who ravaged it. But like the city as a whole, Anderston is slowly recovering, and one hopes that the newcomers to its increasingly upmarket peripheries familiarise themselves with its brief civic motto: *Alter alterius auxilio veget* – 'One flourishes with the help of the other'. No man is an island – even in a riverside penthouse. I'm sure Wee Matt, whom we met at the start of this chapter, would agree.

CHAPTER NINE

Maryhill Unlocked

IN A SUBSEQUENT chapter I suggest that Springburn might be considered the Rome of Glasgow. If the Dear Green Place has a Venice, then it has to be Maryhill. Such a designation will surprise the hordes of commuters from Milngavie who rush the three miles down Maryhill Road to Central Glasgow each day, leaving nothing behind but the pollution from their cars for the local weans to inhale. Many of these car-bound souls have possibly never set foot on *terra firma* between Canniesburn Toll and St George's Cross, the beginning and the end of Maryhill Road. But they are the losers.

Anyone with a bit of knowledge of Maryhill will probably be aware that I am suggesting that it is its position astride the nub of Central Scotland's canal system, where the Forth and Clyde Canal joins the route to Port Dundas in Glasgow, that renders Maryhill the Scottish Venice. It also had its Maryhill Fleet – as its conglomeration of boats at Maryhill Dock was affectionately known – as a rival to the maritime might of the former Doges of Venice. (Ironically, as Maryhill and its industry declined, the term 'Maryhill Fleet' was taken over by one of the gangs that briefly flourished in the area.)

But a minimum of two pieces of evidence is required to make a case for corroboration, and Maryhill has at least such, in that, like Venice, it was also the centre of the glass industry. Indeed, Murano Street, overlooking a canal as important as any in Venice, was named after the Italian city's main glass manufactory. If further proof were needed, Maryhill was the location of one of the most unusual and interesting collections of stained glass in Scotland (*infra*). And then, like Venice with its St Marks, Maryhill had a cathedral. For a while after the Disruption of 1843, the Free Kirkers met in a canalside sawmill at Kelvin Dock with planks for pews, and the place was dubbed by scoffers and mockers 'Maryhill Cathedral'.

I rest my case.

Until the Forth and Clyde Canal came along, there was very little hereabouts apart from the rural estates of several leading Glasgow families – and some light industry such as paper-making along the

River Kelvin. But the Kelvin was soon superseded by the canal, the triumph of the latter symbolised by the mighty Kelvin Aqueduct, built between 1787 and 1790, which carried the canal haughtily over the river on four heavy masonry arches. The Kelvin's water-powered mills were also superseded by the clatter of steam engines as industries migrated to the banks of the new waterway.

The Kelvin Aqueduct was a wonder of the world, perhaps the mightiest aqueduct built since Roman times, and tourists flocked to see it, including crowned heads of Europe. It was the technical key to the Forth and Clyde Canal, itself the artery of the first phase of Scotland's Industrial Revolution. The engineer in charge of its construction was Robert Whitworth and the cost of the structure, at £8,500, almost bankrupted the company building the canal. Scheduled as an Ancient Monument, were this structure in some rural retreat rather than Maryhill, it would be visited by thousands; I doubt if more than a handful of the curious come to see it today. But this may change with the recent reopening of the Forth and Clyde Canal, and the aqueduct could again become a major tourist attraction. One thing that is needed is a poll of the trees that have grown up to obscure any decent view of the aqueduct. Glasgow Council says it is up to Scottish Canals, they say it is up to the council and both seem to be running scared of the tree-hugger lobby.

Maryhill was a wild place in the early years of the Industrial Revolution, and an area of the town consisting of lodging houses and public houses was known as the Botany (*Butney* in local parlance and today commemorated in an eatery called The Butney Bite). This area was possibly so-called as it produced so many souls destined for transportation to Botany Bay. The formation of the first Temperance Society in the world in Maryhill in 1824 by John Dunlop apparently did little to curb excessive drinking (it was a fairly lenient organisation in that it pledged abstinence from spirits, but allowed beer and wine). The nature of the work in constructing the canals, and then the railways, and then later still the waterworks to Glasgow from Loch Katrine which passed though the area, meant that large numbers of Irish navvies were drawn to Maryhill. When they over-refreshed themselves, the local Irish priest would enter the hostelries with a shillelagh and beat about his compatriots until they left the pub. This was dramatic but insufficient law enforcement, and when Glasgow refused to supply a couple of policemen, locals felt they had to act, and police powers were sought – often the main motive for acquiring

Maryhill

Maryhill Route Summary

1   Take a train to Maryhill station.

2   Walk down Maryhill Road and through the 1970s blight created for a road which never was built to the Maryhill Locks and Kelvin Aqueduct.

3   Gain the towpath, cross the canal at the White House, then continue down the canal bank, which gives a wonderful vantage point until Ruchill Street (be careful at Stockingfield Junction not to take the Forth and Clyde Canal; stay on the Glasgow branch).

4   Possible refreshments at Ruchill Church Halls and delight at the Mackintosh-designed architecture.

5   Work your way back up Maryhill Road, passing the Soldiers' Home on the right and the former barracks on the left, and then the restored Burgh Halls at Gairbraid Street.

6   Soon the White House looms into view. Return to the railway station from here, considering refreshments at The Butney Bite.

Approximate route time: 3 hours

burgh status. These powers were attained in 1856 and the town took its name by combining the forename and surname of the wife of a former proprietor of the local Gairbraid estate.

These police powers may have helped clean up the town of undesirable aliens, but new dangers soon arose from within Maryhill and Glasgow itself. The City Council condemned the:

> … inadequate provision now made for the preservation of the Public Peace in this City on those occasions of Riot and Tumult which too frequently occur in the manufacturing and populous districts from a temporary stagnation in trade and want of employment of the working classes.

Despite the fact that Maryhill was an independent burgh, it agreed to the erection of Glasgow's new barracks, which were moved to Maryhill from the East End. The greatly enlarged complex was opened in 1876.

Mainly locally recruited, and the base of the Highland Light Infantry (HLI) from 1920, the soldiers at Maryhill Barracks were deemed to be unreliable during the 1919 40-hour general strike in Glasgow, and were confined to barracks while troops from elsewhere were brought in to re-impose order. The barracks gave Maryhill the air of a military town; there was a Soldiers' Hotel (now a pub/nightclub), a social centre for the soldiery, where those on leave could entertain relatives, and military pubs such as the HLI (now gone) and the Elephant and Bugle (the HLI emblem). Much of the wall of the barracks remains, as does the gatehouse, which gives entry to the Wyndford housing estate that replaced it. The Barracks may not be the Venice Arsenale, but the locals were so attached to the gatehouse that they thwarted plans to demolish it. The Soldiers' Hotel became the Maryhill Trades Union Centre for a while and boasts a mural of the whipping of the leader of the 1797 Weavers' Strike through Glasgow. But Maryhill has its own working-class martyr.

In 1834 there was a strike in the calico printing works. The printers replied to the introduction of blackleg labour by sabotage, destroying their work by tearing it or pouring dye on it. The mill manager was entering the works one day when a pile of bricks and a window frame fell near him. They 'maun jist hae tumbl't oot themsel's,' said the strikers. Arrests were made, some workers jailed and troops from Glasgow Barracks were quartered in the works, where the scabs lived and ate for the duration of the strike.

The authorities were then faced with the murder of a striker in the Butney by 'Clay Davie,' a nab or nob (blackleg). The police investigation was carried out, but the murderer was discharged. The Calico Printers' Union erected a memorial to the worker in Maryhill Churchyard, an iron pillar with a brass inscription:

> To the memory of George Millar, who was mortally wounded at the age of nineteen on the 24 February 1834, by one of those put to the Calico Printing Trade for the purpose of destroying a Union of the regular workmen, formed to protect their wages. This monument was erected by his fellow operatives.

Many of the graves in the churchyard were desecrated by the over-enthusiastic demolition squad, who flattened them into the general rubble when the church itself was demolished, but Millar's was put into storage. It is hoped that Millar's monument might find a home within the former Maryhill Burgh Halls, now restored to their former glory.

Two years after the barracks opened, so did the Municipal Burgh Halls, designed in a revivalist French Renaissance style by David McNaughton. Maryhill has not the richness of public buildings that areas like Govan or Bridgeton possess, so it is fitting that its municipal buildings are amongst the finest of all the burghs that were absorbed by Glasgow. Or were the finest, for shortly after celebrating the centenary of Maryhill's annexation by Glasgow in 1891, the halls were closed. So too was the swimming pool, whose marvelous exterior stretched back from the Burgh Halls.

The crowning glory of the Burgh Halls was a series of 20 stained glass windows made by the Glasgow firm of Stephen Adam. These windows commemorate the industries of Maryhill, and the men and women who worked in them. This in turn gives us the key to Maryhill – its industrial diversity. Govan was ships, Springburn was locomotives, Bridgeton was textiles followed by heavy engineering, but Maryhill had a varied industrial base, recorded in these windows. The rest depict blacksmiths, carpenters, a gas worker, engineers and many other occupations. This is a unique collection of world historic significance, on a par with Maryhill's other great asset, the Kelvin Aqueduct.[1]

Despite its character as an industrial city, public art in Glasgow largely ignores labour as a theme. Where it is recorded, labour is most often represented by classical maidens as at the Stock Exchange, or by Mossman's medievalised workers on the City Chambers, or even by cherubim operating machinery. Adam's Maryhill stained glass panels are a dramatic exception, but there are others. MacGillivray's shipyard workers outside the Govan yard spring to mind (see Chapter 4).

After a long campaign of action and fundraising, the Burgh Halls has been fully restored as providing both social provision and workspaces, and ten of the stained glass panels have been reinstated in the main hall. The swimming pool has also been restored in the adjacent building with which the halls share a common courtyard entrance. Usage of both facilities has exceeded all expectations, showing how badly missed and how needed they were to the local community. The main other building of note hereabouts is the public library on the facing side of Maryhill Road, built in 1905, as were so many others in Glasgow, with help from Andrew Carnegie. It has fine sculptures and a separate entrance for Boys and Girls. The architect was JR Rhind, who designed six of Glasgow's finest libraries at that time.

---

1 An extended account of these artworks is given in the chapter 'Stephen Adam's Stained Glass Workers,' in my *A Glasgow Mosaic; Explorations around the City's Urban Icons* (2013).

In his interesting book *Memories of Maryhill* (1997), Roderick Williamson tells of his interwar childhood, growing up in Braeside Street, amongst the respectable working classes, adding that gangs, violence and criminality were markedly absent from this area of No Mean City – as was sectarianism. Many of the local men were skilled tradesmen with the council, and Wilkinson's father was unique in being an often-unemployed shipwright – and fervent communist. This was the most respectable part of Maryhill, at the very edge of the historical burgh and bordering on posh North Kelvinside. Jock Nimlin, the greatest of the working-class Glasgow mountaineers, also came from hereabouts. His family were Finnish immigrants, Methodists and ILP members, and Jock worked in the shipyards for many years, before writing and radio work led to a job with the National Trust. Let's start here, for just across Maryhill Road is Charles Rennie Mackintosh's Queen's Cross Church, built in 1899 and the only church Mackintosh designed that was actually built. Today it is the headquarters of the Mackintosh Society, and is open to visitors at certain times.

As you proceed northwards up Maryhill Road, you can understand why churches like Queen's Cross were closed, for between here and the junction with Queen Margaret Drive much of the original housing has been demolished, to be replaced by 'landscaped' areas, dead land covered with supermarket trolleys, rubbish and dogshit. Signs are, however, that living beside the canal is now being seen as a plus, and new apartments are being built along its banks. From Queen Margaret Drive to Ruchill Street, Maryhill Road retains its original unbroken tenement line, and Ruchill Street itself has a Mackintosh connection, in that the Church Halls, where you can drop in for a cup of tea and a keek, are his work – though not the church itself. This is still the heart of an active congregation that has a deep social commitment to the local community, and if they are able to show you round, make a contribution to the maintenance of the building.

Further up the road we are in the heart of present-day Maryhill, with the site of the barracks on the left. Their wall is now overtowered by the multi-storey flats that replaced it in the Wyndford housing scheme. When built, this was one of the biggest estates outside of the four peripheral Glasgow schemes such as Castlemilk, and it won a Saltire Award for its design. The Wyndford is still a well-kept estate with a good sense of community. Indeed, when it was suggested that the Barracks Wall be demolished to unite the Wynford with the rest of Maryhill, the residents rose up in arms against the planned destruction of their comfortable mental horizons. It has been proposed as a Conservation Area, which might make it the first 1960s housing scheme to be awarded the accolade.

Passing the Burgh Halls on the left, and then an aqueduct that carries the canal over the road, you come to the part of Maryhill most associated with the waterway. On the left are soon seen Maryhill docks, locks and dry dock – with the associated Kelvin Aqueduct – one of the biggest complexes of canal construction associated with the entire feat of engineering a canal across Scotland. Still standing too is The White House, a pub dating from the days of canal construction, but last a public house back in the 1980s. This fine wee building has recently had a makeover with essential repairs being carried out, and has opened as a furniture showroom. However, a canalbank hostelry built for those using the waterway, which had a 24-hour licence to deal with the constant canal traffic, has long gone. A modern bungalow stands on the site of the former lock-keeper's cottage. Work here for the keeper was intermittent, and even in the 1920s the lock-keeper, John Smith, kept a few cows grazing on the lockside pastures and produced milk to supplement his income. I had a communication from a woman in Canada whose grandmother, as the eldest of nine children, had had the job of delivering the milk from this wee farm of the lock-keeper's before her school started. As a result she was often late for school and belted, and her younger brother would offer to take the strap in her place. This gallant lad ran away at 16, though underage, to fight in the Great War; he was killed after a week at the front.

The reopening of the canal will hopefully be a focus for the regeneration of the whole area around Maryhill Locks. Plans for a marina and associated housing, even possibly a hotel, were mooted for the locks area, but these have evaporated with the current economic crisis. However, landscaped and restored as a working canal, things here are a great improvement to the utter dereliction that used to be. But not further up Maryhill Road, alas.

I was looking across northwards to the desolation still there from the 1970s when the tenements on both sides of Maryhill Road – including the absolutely splendid Maryhill Cross building with its fine ogee roof, featured in various photographs and even a wartime painting of the docks – were demolished for a dual carriageway built to speed the burghers of Bearsden and Milngavie into their work in Glasgow; insult was added to injury in that this road was never constructed, but the desolation remains. Up came a punter who pointed

to the boarded up building which had contained the Redan public
house.

'It wis named aifter a battle in the Crimean War. The lads in the
Maryhill Barracks gied it that name aifter they cam back.'

I thanked my informant for the information, not pointing out to
him that the Crimean War took place 25 years before the Maryhill
Barracks were built – and thus possibly discouraging his interest in
matters historical.

On 26 May 2001 a fleet of 40 vessels sailed from Falkirk to
Bowling, ceremonially reopening the canal. Now holiday operators
are offering barge cruises from Glasgow to Falkirk – or all the way to
Edinburgh. This is a revival of the use the folk of Maryhill traditionally put the canal to. Their 'doon the watter' was a cruise, in boats
like the *Gypsy Queen*, which ran from 1905 to 1940, along the canal
to Kilsyth or further, with jazz bands playing. Until the closure of the
canal in 1962, the weans of Maryhill would help the yachtsmen and
fishermen who latterly frequented it to open the various lock gates,
and as reward hitch a lift as far as Clydebank or even Bowling. It is
unlikely, however, that any hitched a lift on the midget submarine that
negotiated the canal in 1952.

Maryhill Dock is a good point to transfer from Maryhill Road
to the canal banks, and retrace steps south, ending up almost where
we started. Landscaped, cleaned up and devoted to leisure pursuits,
the canal still shows the evidence of its past as the industrial artery
of Scotland, and of Maryhill in particular. The economic life of the
burgh was so varied that pointing out a few of the more prominent
factories, or their remains, is the best policy. The locks at Maryhill
had a dock slipway, still visible, where boat building and repair took
place between 1857 and the 1950s. The firm of Swan built many of
the famous Clyde 'Puffers,' the iron-hulled and steam propeller driven
vessels which plied the canal and the Firth of Clyde, including the very
first one, the *Glasgow*. The dock is still commemorated in the stub of a
pub opposite (its tenement gone), called The Kelvin Dock. Swan, who
became the first Provost of Maryhill, recruited many of his skilled men
from amongst Falkirk's ironworkers.

On the right, heading towards Glasgow from the White House,
there is a hill. Here Swan the Provost had his mansion, appropriately
named *Collina*, before pollution – partly from his own nearby spleter
(zinc) works – drove him to the suburbs of Maryhill Park. This area is
now ironically called The Valley and is in the process of having a

whole new social housing project built on its slopes. Originally tenements here, these were demolished and replaced by some low quality
council housing in the 1920s. In the 1930s the population was largely
unemployed, stayed in bed till noon, and the area was dubbed 'Happy
Valley' by outsiders. Happy it possibly was not, but today it still
remains the only hill in Glasgow that is a valley.

As the canal snakes towards Glasgow, the main branch heads from
the Stockingfield Junction towards Falkirk. A confused jumble of
buildings now occupy the ground of the former Kelvin, later Maryhill,
Iron Works, behind which lies the stadium – if that is not too grand a
statement – of Maryhill FC. Maryhill FC engage in a sport bearing
some resemblance to football, and has produced such greats as Danny
McGrain from their ranks – though the last time they won the Junior
Cup was in 1940. The Maryhill Harriers still operate, and, though like
the Juniors, their great days are in the past, they have produced three
Olympic competitors, and a marathon gold medalist at the first Empire
Games in 1930, 'Dunkie' Wright. The most popular sport amongst the
locals would appear to be fishing in the canal. I asked one if he ever
caught anything and whether it was fit to eat. 'Oh aye,' he said, 'Ah
get a lot o pike. Bit ah never eat it. Ah hate fish.' As you proceed, there
is a culvert on your right leading water from the canal to the site of the
former works. Till about 1860, when the burgh raised money from the
rates for a sewage system, this was Maryhill's main source of water, of
washing, and of its sewage disposal, leading to outbreaks of cholera,
typhus and typhoid, which killed hundreds.

On the left now appears the former Bryant and May factory,
which produced Scottish Bluebell matches until 1981, and which itself
was formerly Alexander Fergusson's Lead and Colour Works. This
handsome building, now fronted by a rather faded mural about the
delights of the canal, has been converted to non-industrial use. Passing
the bascule bridge over the canal at Ruchill Street, you have Mackintosh's Ruchill Halls in view again on the right, while on the left is
the site of what was Maryhill's largest industrial undertaking, McLel-
lan's Rubber Works, dating from 1876. This was the biggest industrial
concern in Maryhill with about 2,000 workers; factory growth was
restricted by the canalside location of most of the works. With the
remains of its own canalside wharfs, and working till a few years ago,
McLellans finally closed about ten years ago and the land was sold
for housing. The flats erected here have an Amsterdam canalside feel,
emphasised by their naming after the famous Dutch artist Mondrian

and their copying of his dramatic block colour schemes, which bring cheer on even a gloomy day. These are a great improvement in the visual feel of the canal.

I was lunching in the Mackintosh Ruchill Church Halls one day shortly after these flats had been put on the market, at prices way below West End ones, due to their location. Two lassies with their weans in their buggies (often The Fella That Did It gets away up here) were discussing them, admiring them, and one sadly added, 'See the price! £100,000 – ye would hiv tae be a millionaire tae buy one, a millionaire.' We are producing an increasingly wealth-polarised society where for half the population, that sum would represent a snip at the price, whilst for the other half it remains beyond their wildest dreams.

The canal bends, and soon, on the opposite side where now only coots and swans survey the doings of the coarse anglers by the canal banks, are the sites of the two Maryhill glass factories, the Caledonia Works producing bottles and jars, and the Glasgow Works manufacturing plate glass. Much of this land is now taken up by a Glasgow University student village. Murano Street overlooks the glassworks no more, and the canalside here recently lost its last active industrial unit in McGhee's Bakery, which stood on the site of the former Firhill Sawmills. Again, a new block of flats, pleasant but not up to Mondrian standard, lines the canalside here. The underpassing of the delightfully restored Nolly Brig brings you to Firhill Basin.

On the other side of the canal, within the Ruchill section of the former burgh, are more remains of Maryhill's industrial past. The ironworks of Shaw and MacInnes survived miraculously until the year 2000, and next to that, also on the canal, were found the Phoenix chemical works, not alas rising from the ashes like the mythical bird they were named after. Both works long used the Firhill Basin to transport their products from Maryhill to market. Shaw and MacInnes had originally, like the Swans at Kelvindock, brought their skilled ironworkers from Falkirk; appropriately they came by the canal. It is a pity the works closed, as there has been a great upsurge in the restoration and new casting of ironwork, and the last Scottish firm to do ornamental cast iron work is having difficulty meeting potential orders.

One can take a short walk up to Ruchill Park for a fine view of the city, from its high point, created by building a mini-mountain from the rubble left after the construction of Ruchill Hospital. This, formerly the highest point in Glasgow, used to be known as 'Ben' Whitton, after the then Director of Parks. Or simply head back down to Queen's

Cross Church and our starting point at Burnside Street. By now you will have a good idea of where the inspiration for those stained glass windows in the Burgh Hall came from, and will understand how the Forth and Clyde Canal gave birth to Maryhill. Hopefully in its new-found role as a tourist, wildlife and recreation corridor, the waterway will make a contribution towards Maryhill's regeneration – though the industries of the papermaker, glassblower, chemical worker and all the others have disappeared forever from the canal banks.

I have been fortunate enough to get a feel for Maryhill, in as much as any outsider can hope to really do, from being involved with the work over the years involved in the restoration of the Burgh Halls and in the manifold offshoots to that work in local schools and community associations. Against stereotypes of urban alienation and atomisation, it was clear to me that the area still retained, despite everything, a sense of identity and community, and despite the frequent self-mocking disparagement of Maryhill by its inhabitants as Merry-hell. A few years ago I put several articles about various post-industrial areas of Glasgow on the Glasgow West End Website, and the responses were encouraging – for example, Partick got a full six pages of engaged informative postings. At the current count, Maryhill has over 70 pages of comments – from the area, from the rest of Scotland where some families have moved, and from the wider world of emigration to Canada, Australia and elsewhere. Tales told fondly of the steamie and baths, of the cinema, of the canal and of the HLI and the barracks. Heaven it may never have been, but Glasgow's Venice was far from Hell, merry or otherwise, in the past. And it remains so today – despite everything.

For the Burgh Halls contact 0845 860 1856 or info@mbht.org.uk
Or go to www.maryhillburghhalls.org.uk

The Burgh Halls Trust has produced three excellent walking trails to North, South and Central Maryhill, available as brochures or as downloads.

CHAPTER TEN

Possil: Potemkin Village

A METEORITE FELL on Possil in 1804. Nothing much had happened there before that, and little was to happen for a while thereafter. It is true that the Forth and Clyde Canal had snaked past High Possil at Lambhill in the 1790s, and after curling its way west through Maryhill, turned east at Stockingford Junction and reached Port Dundas, in Low Possil, a decade or so later. But the three miles between Lambhill and Port Dundas remained a rural area till well into the 19th century, with not even a village existing.

Ordnance Survey maps of the 1860s show Possil, then in Lanarkshire, as an area of scattered farms, with some quarries and coal pits with attendant miners' rows. Amongst a few country houses, the most important was Possil House, built in 1710, and attached to which was much of the land hereabouts. Possil briefly became a point on the literary circuit of Europe, when the lease of Possil House was taken in 1835 by Archibald Allison, a senior member of the Scottish judiciary. He held it till his death in 1867. Born in England of Scottish parents, Allison practiced law in Scotland and was involved in many famous trials, from that of Burke the murderer at the beginning of his career to that of Madeleine Smith towards its end. He became Rector of Glasgow University in 1852.

Allison had literary ambitions and wrote a multivolume *History of Europe*, published over a long period, and much of it was written at Possil House. Largely unread today, this was a bestseller at its time, each volume eagerly awaited, and it sold 100,000 copies in Britain and America, as well as being translated into German, French and Arabic. Possil House became a place of pilgrimage, and royalty from Europe, as well as literati such as Charles Dickens, made it a port of call on their trips to Scotland. Allison apparently told Dickens that he had no future as a novelist and should try some other field of literary activity. Visitors found Possil as delightful as did Allison himself. He wrote in his autobiography, *Some Account of My Life and Writings*:

> I was fortunate enough to find Possil House unoccupied and to let furnished; it proved a delightful residence. Situated in a park of 30 acres studded with noble trees, some two centuries old.

Allison also enjoyed his daily walk of three miles each way into Glasgow and back, where he continued to engage in public life; indeed, he walked to Hamilton and back shortly before his death.

Allison's residence at Possil was not completely trouble free. He had been involved in the prosecution of the cotton spinners in 1838, a show trial that does little credit to his reputation for impartiality (see the chapter on Anderston), and like many of his time and class, he was worried by the rebellious condition of the working classes. When in the year of Chartist agitation of 1842 the local miners went on strike, Allison armed his servants and expected Possil House to be attacked. A message from the miners assured him that he was safe. This did not teach Allison much humanity and he imposed savage sentences of transportation on the alleged ringleaders of the Glasgow 'Chartist' Riots in 1848. On his death in 1867, the Possil estate with the mansion house was put up for sale, and the area was to change dramatically.

Walter Macfarlane had been born in Torrance, a few miles north of Possil, but moved to Glasgow and became engaged in the iron-founding trade. At first he set up a foundry in Saracen Street in Calton, but shifted to Anderston in the 1860s as he expanded. There was an insatiable demand for cast iron goods in the later 19th century. Pipes and drains were needed for the expanding programme of sanitation, both domestic and public, parks looked for cast iron fountains to embellish them, and cast iron was used for decoration on buildings in the form of railings, balconies, and canopies. Soon Macfarlane's works at Anderston were too cramped, for the one thing the casting of iron needs is a huge floor space. Macfarlane bought the Possil estate in 1868, and decide to establish what we would now call a green-field site and garden suburb for his workers.

Macfarlane lived in a magnificent house in Glasgow's Park Circus and, having no need for Possil House, he demolished it, though it is commemorated today in Mansion Street. The new foundry was built in two years and opened in 1870, covering a site of 14 acres. Its front-age was an elaborate design featuring much cast iron, advertising its products. Macfarlane built canopies for banks and botanical gardens, as well as railway stations, specialising in large-scale construction works at the top end of the market. Central Station in Glasgow, where he built the canopy for carriages, is possibly his best local work, and many of the park fountains in the city (see Chapter 12) are his. His nephew of the same name took over the business on his uncle's death in 1885, and by the 1890s, 1,200 men were labouring in the Saracen. It was

Possil

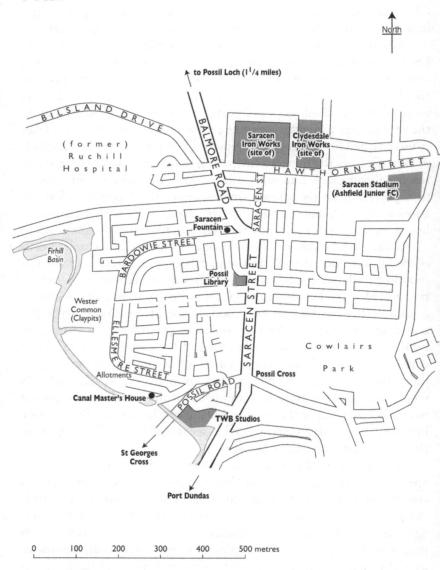

Possil Route Summary

1 Badly served by transport as Possil is, you must get yourself somehow to Possil Basin to begin this route.

2 Cross the canal at Canal House and walk up Ellesmere Street, past the allotments and Westercommon.

3 Head down Bardowie Road to Saracen Cross at the Fountain.

4 Walk up Saracen Street to the one-time site of the Saracen Foundry, now that of Allied Vehicles, a Possil success story.

5 Hawthorn Street takes you to Saracen Stadium, from where you can wander and wend your way back though the acres of emptiness to Saracen Street and the library.

6 Go down Saracen Street to Possil Cross.

7 Continue down Possil Road and beneath the canal to near where you began the walk.

Approximate route time: 2.5 hours

world-famous, and the Saracen gained orders from Valparaiso to Vancouver. Its 2,000-page, two-volume catalogue was a work of art in itself, listing 6,000 items available from the foundry. *Macfarlane's Castings* has recently been republished in a limited edition by a fine art society in the US. There was little interest in Macfarlane in this country after the Possil works closed and was demolished, but things are beginning to change. Recently some paving stones in a domestic garden were upturned to reveal the printing blocks from one of Macfarlane's catalogues; they have been brought for about £2,000 and will help with educational and restorative work in the current cast iron revival.

Macfarlane was politically prominent in Glasgow, helping found the Liberal Association in 1879, and becoming a firm supporter of Gladstone's reforming policies. He died leaving a personal fortune of £100,000, aside from the value of the firm and its works themselves. Interestingly, his nephew, in changing times, became a Liberal Unionist, opposing Gladstone's policy of Home Rule for Ireland. Macfarlane was an art collector at his home in Park Circus, which his nephew extensively remodeled in a late high Victorian style. This building has undergone various changes of use, being for a while the Glasgow Registry Offices. The house features much cast iron work, including the elaborate conservatory to the rear made by Macfarlane himself, with Adam stained glass inlays.

From almost nothing, Possilpark's population had grown to 10,000 by the 1890s, but this was not solely due to Macfarlane. Possil became the centre for iron founding as a whole, and had no fewer than five operating foundries before 1914. The Clydesdale Iron Works stood just east of the Saracen works. To the south in Denmark Street were the Keppoch Iron works and the Possil Iron Works, their demolished sites still vacant. And to the north, at the canal at Strachur Street were the Lambhill Iron Works, which also employed about 1,000 men. But these other works were largely involved in the mass production of cheaper castings, gutters, drains and such like, and it was the Saracen which raised cast iron work to an art form, and whose reputation deservedly survives. It is possible that the proximity of the canal, bringing pig iron from Lanarkshire, was the reason for Possil becoming the centre of the cast iron industry, or possibly Macfarlane's success there just encouraged others to follow.

Some other interesting industries came to Possil, such as the Nautilus Pottery Works, whose fine ware is now collectible. They closed in 1948. The Workshops for the Blind opened in 1927, but have also since departed. But Possil was basically a foundry town, and it prospered while the demand for cast iron was insatiable. However, tastes changed, and the fashion for ornate cast iron did not survive the First World War. Later, other materials came along, like plastics for piping, which were cheaper, lighter and more durable. Significantly, the Lambhill Iron Works closed as early as 1920. The others continued, struggling to adapt and being helped by rearmament work during the Second World War. But, constantly reducing in scale, the industry finally died in the 1960s, and the Saracen itself closed in 1965, five years short of its centenary. Possil suffered. It was known originally as a high-wage area with good quality housing, and even between the wars the overspill areas from its core, such as Hamiltonhill, boasted quality corporation dwellings, and a Senior Secondary School built in 1933. A former pupil of this now demolished school, Willy Maley – whose father fought in the Spanish Civil War – is Professor of Renaissance Studies at Glasgow University. Today Possil is one of the areas of the city most ravaged by unemployment, poverty and drugs, and, sadly – crime. Possil's chances of producing another Glasgow University professor are probably less than previously.

Possil Road goes under a rather forbidding canal aqueduct to enter the territory, so let's take the scenic route to Possil. Heading up the remaining granite setts of Baird's Brae, you come to the towpath of the Glasgow branch of the Forth and Clyde Canal, which leads to Spiers Wharf and Port Dundas. From the later 18th century until closure in the 1950s, this was a port for much of Glasgow's trade, especially for the distilleries roundabouts, and at Spiers Wharf are what must be some of the most splendid warehouses anywhere, like Adam mansions, now mainly converted into flats. Swans nest where the barges once emptied their cargoes of grain.

Across the canal bascule (lifting) footbridge at Possil Basin are the offices of the British Waterways Board, with a collection of aquatic craft moored there, and the basin's quay has some quaint workshops dating from the time of the canal's construction. Sadly boarded up and unoccupied is the former canal master's house, a small gem that might have, with imagination, been restored as offices for Scottish Canals instead of them building the unsightly modern premises that stands here. On the opposite bank of the canal is a huge wild area, a sight of scenic beauty, give or take a few wrecked cars and supermarket trolleys. You discover the method of gaining access to this wild area, and make other discoveries in the process, when you head up Applecross Street for Hamiltonhill, moving along Ellesmere Street. Immediately you encounter a level of deprivation that is almost third world, and here we have the headquarters of Emmaus, Glasgow, which works with homeless and marginalised people in a recycling charity project. They are needed in Possil.

Glasgow may now aspire to be Britain's second shopping city, but not here, not in Hamiltonhill, where four of the six shops in the local shopping centre are closed, boarded up and for let. How do people here purchase the necessities of life? One possible answer is given by the allotments on Ellesmere Street, still bravely tended and producing vegetables – and social interaction. The guys working there were quite willing to chat and show me around. 'It's no sae much for the vegetables, we gie maist of them awye. It's tae pass the time and get oot the hoose,' said one of my hosts. On a recent visit I found these allotments part-deserted and overgrown. The site had been closed due to fears of soil contamination, and was later re-opened but has yet to regain its former glory.

Another surprise lies further on at Westercommon, whose location was indicated by a just-legible, fire-damaged sign. Braving the entrance, which was cunningly camouflaged to look like a rubbish coup, I entered. The common has the best view of Glasgow from any-where, one to die for; the city looks like Florence – well, a wee bit – with the Italianate towers of Park Circus in the middle foreground.

Westercommon is what is left of Glasgow's once extensive common lands, where inhabitants had the right to graze cattle, which were driven out through Cowcaddens to pasture. The city's population also had the right to quarry building stone and collect turf and wood for fuel. From the Clyde at Partick these lands stretched to Possil, but much was sold off to pay Glasgow's debts in the 18th century, after the Shawfield Riots of 1725 against the malt tax. In clashes with troops, eight rioters had been killed at the Shawfield Mansion in Glasgow. This was the home of Duncan Campbell, MP for the city, and suppos-edly a supporter of the malt tax. The government wanted the council to take action against the rioters, but instead the baillies started to proceed against the military authorities for murder. Some council members were arrested when General Wade, no less, was sent to the city to restore order.

The Glasgow authorities' ill-disguised support for these riots against the malt tax led to a heavy fine being imposed on the city, while many rioters were flogged, imprisoned or banished. In subsequent (rather shady) deals, the Glasgow city authorities somewhat under-mined their heroic stand over the Shawfield Riots. After paying the fine through the sale of the common lands, most of what was left was divided up between the grasping baillies for nominal sums. All that remains now is several acres of wild land sloping down to the canal.

I was glad to see that the citizens of Glasgow are still insisting on their common rights, at least here in Hamiltonhill. Apart from using it as a place for building their corrugated iron pigeon lofts, modern versions of the old Scottish dookit, and as an unofficial kids' scramble bike track, the locals have formed the Friends of Possilpark Greens-pace to help maintain and improve the common. Here is a wetland, a reeded habitat by the canal supporting a great variety of waterfowl, swans, coots, widgeon and tufted duck – and pigeons from the lofts on the bank, as well as a herd of roe deer. Firhill Basin, with the removal of canal bridges, now boasts an artificial island and protected nesting site. An urban forest and wetland in one, and a resource for the local people, very few of who belong to the car owning class that can escape easily to the countryside. Access to a car is often used as a poverty index. At one household in ten, Possil's car access rate is the lowest in the UK.

From Westercommon can be seen to advantage the A-listed tower of the former Ruchill Hospital (in Possil) next to Ruchill Park (Maryhill). This was Glasgow's fever hospital, and the grounds were scheduled for a housing development, one of many that have not materialised. The hospital continues to decay, but the Tower remains. On the northern side of the hospital on Bilsland Drive are some of the grand former residences for doctors and nurses; these have been sold off for private housing, although the former hospital laundry has been made into social housing, as part of the Possil Corridor improvement.

Heading down Ellesmere Street and Bardowie Street, you pass much cleared and derelict land, full of rubbish and weeds, as you get towards Saracen Street, where at Saracen Cross you are in the heart of Possil. At the street's north end is a small Macfarlane fountain, with the message 'Keep the Pavement Dry'. I was reflecting that this, and the land for the library, was the sum of Macfarlane's beneficence to Possil, when I was interrupted. In Possil of all places, where nobody goes, you are visible as an outsider, but my interest in the fountain probably indicated that I was neither a social security investigator nor, worse still, an arm of the law. Bob and I got quite pally and we went for a drink, at his request, after our chat. It went something like this:

Bob: 'Aye, he gave a lot tae Possil did Macfarlane.'

Me: 'But he took a lot mair oot.'

Bob: 'You're a smart bugger, eh? Aye, right enough, so he did. Used tae be a great place, Possil, but it's got a bad reputation noo, and it deserves it tae. Ah served ma time in the Saracen, but I didnae like it and shifted tae the distillery at Port Dundas. That started ma problems. Ah'm an alcoholic noo. Ye fancy buyin me a pint?'

As we entered the pub I heard one woman shout to another:

'Hey, Jeannie, the Housing Association says ye've tae pit curtains up, in case the kids think yer hoose is unoccupied and fling bricks at the windaes.'

And thus I learned there was an ethical code governing 'daein in windaes' in Possil.

I somewhat scandalised Bob by refusing to join him in a pint at 11.30am and, after settling him down, carried on with my travels along Saracen Street. At first sight, this street is appealing, if lacking in great architectural merit. There are few gap sites (the main one is now currently being in-filled with a 'Health' Centre) and the shops are occupied, if not selling many luxury items, the pubs are still there, as is the Co-op building and the Lido 'Tally' Café – much as it would have been 50 to 100 years ago, and there is a healthy bustle. But Saracen Street is like those Potemkin Villages built for Catherine the Great in Russia, which had nothing behind the main street. For to the east and west of Saracen Street lie what must be the most extensive brownfield sites in Glasgow, acre after acre of flattened, derelict and overgrown land. A start has been made in building new, low-rise housing, north of the grandly named Cowlairs Park, which is nothing but an abandoned set of former football pitches. But it is difficult to see where the population will come from to fill these wastes, whose extent is revealed by taking a side walk from here towards Saracen Park, home of Ashfield Juniors FC, at the north-east corner of Possil and back along Hawthorn Street.

It is worth visiting Possil Library. The land was given by Macfarlane, the construction funded by a Carnegie grant, and the building opened in 1913. Its most interesting features are six interior murals done by final-year students of the Glasgow School of Art that year. These represent Geography, Art, Science and so forth, and are attractive, if conventional. Commerce is, as usual, represented by classical maidens. The library contains what is probably the only known photograph of the Saracen Iron Works (drawings exist), taken in the 1960s just before demolition. Further down the street is an interesting small office building announcing that it belonged to Gavin Watson Printers, founded in 1863, but sadly closed in 2006.

At the bottom of Saracen Street is Possil Cross, which was destroyed by redevelopment. Attempts have been made, by building new flats at a couple of its corners, to bring back a focus to the area. Heading down Possil Road towards the aqueduct, an old whisky bond has been converted into artists' studios at TWB and is a striking red brick addition to the skyline, replacing the former Rockvilla School that once stood here high on its eminence. You can still find the separate Boys and Girls stairs which led up from the street to the school, if you look hard enough on the east side of Possil Road.

The basic problem in areas like Possil is that a lifestyle has emerged and we are now into its third generation. The grandfathers lost their jobs, the fathers didn't work and now these in turn have produced kids. Unemployment in areas like Possil is probably three times the official figure; to that should be added those on disability benefits, and those, like unmarried mothers, on social security, neither of who count in the unemployment totals. In Glasgow as a whole, it is estimated that 25 per cent of those of employment age are not working. Either they are unemployed, on sickness or disability benefits, or on social security. In areas like Possil the figure is safely double that. There are few jobs for the people in Possil and they have not the skills or means to obtain work elsewhere. But they have learned to survive, on benefits supplemented by the black economy. And the ones who escape this poverty of ambition are the criminals and drug dealers.

But there is a shining example of an exception to the rule. If you carry on up north from Saracen Cross, Saracen Street takes you to Hawthorn Street, where Macfarlane's works and other iron-works were situated. This is the current manufacturing location for Allied Vehicles, which was started 20 years ago in a local adjacent disused cinema, and which now employs 450 workers making taxis and adapting vehicles for disabled use as well as manufacturing a wide range of disabled accessories. The firm has a policy, where possible, of employing and training local people, giving the lie to those who say the unemployed would not work even if work were available. And Allied Vehicles is going from strength to strength.

Northwards again from here takes you through an area of Possil that is mainly inter-war housing rather than tenemented. Sadly it is hereabouts that the local crime families, mafias who prey on and add to misery, have their operations. Soon afterwards, Balmore Road drops down to the canal and the jewel in Possil's crown, Possil Loch, which is a Site of Scientific Interest, a wetland that is a migratory refuge for many birds, and which has a fine circular walk around it. You can pick up a walking trail to this, and other walks in the area, at the Lambhill Stables, a building that was reduced to a ruin but has been restored as a community hub with café, garden and a wee museum, as well as being a centre for music and repairing bikes, amongst other things. It also has a trail to the site of the nearby Cadder Pit Disaster of 1913, in which 22 men were killed, and leaflets explaining the surrounding circumstances. Like Allied Vehicles, Lambhill Stables is a success story in what might otherwise be seen as an unrelenting picture of grimness in Possil.

Possil lacks the profile that some other parts of the city have – apart from in respect of its drug wars. There are no books on Possil, no autobiographies of life there (since no one famous came from Possil, apart from Lena Martell, the jazz singer). It doesn't feature large in histories of the city, since even its main industry seems to have been forgotten in a way that shipbuilding and railway construction have not. Poor Possil. Let's transpose to it a refrain originally describing Camlachie, an area which now no longer exists, and which, despite everything, I'm sure still expresses the feelings of many of Possil's remaining inhabitants:

> Oh Possil, oh Possil, oh Possil my ain
> I love each dirty windae, each broken doon stane.

For information on, or to help with, Westercommon aka The Claypits, contact:
www.tinyurl.com/claypits

Lambhill Stables can be contacted at 0141 945 4100 and information is available at www.lambhillstables.org

CHAPTER ELEVEN

Springburn: Rome of the North

Born Balgrayhill Schooled Petershill
Worked Keppochhill Married Springburnhill
Sick Stobhill Domiciled Barnhill
Rested Sighthill.

SPRINGBURN – the Rome of the North? Consider the evidence. Like Rome, Glasgow's Springburn is built on seven hills, as the above ditty records. And the Romans were there – in fact they built the Antonine Wall just to the north of Springburn, and through the area a Roman road went to the fort on the wall at Cadder.

But most tellingly, just as in the days of the Roman Empire, when 'all roads led to Rome,' so at the height of the British Empire, all roads, or at least the vital iron ones, led to Springburn. The British Empire was held together by its railways, and before 1914 more than half of the locomotives riding the lines of mother country and colonies were built in Springburn. As Govan was the world capital of shipbuilding, Springburn was the world capital of locomotive building. From the workshops there, the trains were trundled down the tramlines at night to the docks, and thence were carried by sea to all parts of the globe. These events were marked by the local population, who poured out under the gas streetlamps to watch the mighty engines rolling by.

In Springburn Park there stands, like a memorial to a Roman emperor, the statue of James Reid. From the highest hill in Glasgow, he looks down over the district that was his empire, and whose character he did so much to forge. Born in Auchterarder in 1823, Reid became a partner in, and manager of, the Hydepark Works, which he bought over in 1876, bringing his sons into the business. Before he died in 1894, Reid had left his mark on Springburn – and on Glasgow itself. Springburn Park opened in 1892, and the following year Reid gifted it a bandstand, constructed by MacFarlane's Saracen Foundry in Possil. Reid's statue was erected in the park in 1900, and commemorated his role both as President of the Society of Engineers and Shipbuilders, and President of the Royal Glasgow Institute of Fine Arts. The family were art collectors, and a fine portrait of James Reid hangs in Glasgow

Springburn

Springburn Route Summary

1 Despite Springburn's harsh treatment this is a great walk. Take a train to Springburn station, then walk up Springburn Way to Balgrayhill Road (Mackintosh villas).

2 At Springburn Park, take the Mosesfield House (possible view of Ben Lomond here), Reid's statue and Winter Gardens circuit, then exit near Breezes Tower.

3 Walk down Balgrayhill Road (where much of *Red Road* was filmed – and you can see why!) to Atlas Road, Atlas Square and Flemington Street (North British Locomotive Company offices).

4 Consider refreshments if the college opposite is open.

5 Continue back across Springburn Road and round to have a look at Springburn's Broken Heart.

6 From here, go downhill to Sighthill Cemetery and the Martyrs' Memorial.

7 Barnhill station is a bit closer than Springburn station for the return journey.

Approximate route time: 3 hours

Kelvingrove Galleries, to which they also gifted a Constable, a Corot and a Turner.

James's son, Hugh, left an even bigger mark on Springburn and especially on its fine park. He purchased the mansion and grounds of Mosesfield in 1904 and donated these to the park. In Mosesfield mansion in 1896, George Johnston created the prototype of the Arrol-Johnston motor car and laid the foundation of the Scottish automobile industry. Thus in Springburn, at the height of the boom in the railways, was invented the vehicle that would lead to the sad demise of the iron ways. After a while as Springburn Museum, Mosesfield mansion became an old men's club, which it remains.

His own mansion, Belmont House, was built in 1889 by Hugh Reid on his marriage and in its day was both the largest and the highest house (at 350 feet above sea level) in Glasgow, with a view from its eminence overlooking seven counties. When he died in 1935, he left the building for use as a children's home. Unfortunately, after a while as a training school for nurses and as administrative buildings for Stobhill

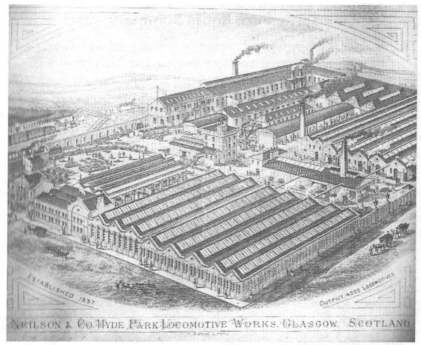

Hyde Park Works: A fine drawing of the works from the same time as the 1891 strike. Founded by Neilson and later owned by Reid, when it amalgamated with the Atlas Works across the tracks in 1903, it produced the largest railway-building complex on earth.

Hospital, Belmont was demolished in 1985. Other features in the park recalling Hugh Reid are the Unicorn Column, a pottery monument supplied by Doulton of Lambeth; this was originally erected elsewhere but has been in the park since 1970. Its formerly vandalised unicorn has now been restored to the top of the column. Alas, the beast's horn has once again vanished. Hugh also donated £10,000 in 1900 to the now derelict but once magnificent Winter Gardens in the park; there is talk of restoration here. The splendid rockery remains open, however.

In the era when, apart from the summer holiday, most working people found their recreational opportunities limited to the local public park, the area reflected many of the aspects of the social values the upper classes sought to impose on the lower orders. Within the park's bounds, approved uplifting recreational activities took place, as did approved entertainment. They were closed on Sundays and no alcohol was sold. The parks frequently hosted war memorials emphasising the duty of loyalty to King and Country, and statues of civic

dignitaries, often local capitalists, recording their benevolence. Springburn Park is a fine example of the park as a value system.

The basis of this Reid family largesse was the enormous wealth
generated by locomotive manufacture before 1914. Before air and
even road were serious rivals to its transport monopoly, the possession
of a worldwide Empire provided a captive market for steam railway
engines. Hugh Reid astutely brought about the end of competition
between the Glasgow-based locomotive manufacturers in 1903
through an amalgamation of the Hydepark with its main rivals, the
Atlas Works and Queen's Park Works, to form the North British
Locomotive Works. From being a sleepy weavers' village in the 1840s,
Springburn by 1900 was the main centre of world locomotive making,
with up to 15,000 people working in the railway factories and associated railway yards at peak times.

Springburn's advantages turned into disadvantages. Its factories
continued to mass-produce steam locomotives for a diminishing
Empire and a diminishing captive market. The general manager of the
NBLC predicted in 1936 that electricity would never replace steam on
main-line trains, so innovation stagnated. By the time the Glasgow
works switched to diesel and, later, electric locomotives, they were
unable to compete. Locomotive production stopped in Springburn in
the 1960s. An ever-shrinking BREL repair workshop facility at Cowlairs
continued as the area's main link with its glorious industrial past,
until it was closed with the loss of 1,600 jobs in 1986. Today about
150 workers remain at the Alston depot in the former St Rollox railway
works, repairing railway carriages. You can see many fine specimens
of Springburn's craftsmanship in the Glasgow Riverside Museum.

Unlike some other industrial areas of Glasgow, which were almost
entirely working class, Springburn had a more complex class structure,
and Balgrayhill, in which the park was situated, was then the desirable part of Springburn. Aside from Mosesfield mansion and the 'wee
hoose above the shop' i.e. Reid's Belmont mansion to the north of the
park, the southern park boundary was formed by Broomfield Road, a
street of solid if modest middle-class villas. This 'posh' bit of Springburn even has a 'castle' in the form of Balgray Tower. Locally known
as Breezes Tower, this is a mock-Tudor house built in the 1830s, with
a three-storey central octagonal tower and is still functioning as a
dwelling house. Urban myths are fascinating. I was studying the tower
when a proud local came up and claimed, 'It was built by a tobacco
lord, for tae see his ships comin up the Clyde'. I didn't have the heart

to point out the tobacco lords were long gone by 1830, and I left him with his comforting myth.

But he was right when he told me, to my initial scepticism, 'And there's a Rennie Mackintosh hoose just doon below it'. At 140–2 Balgrayhill Road is indeed a two-storey semi-detached villa that was designed for a relative by Charles Rennie Macintosh in 1890. Its semi-octagonal bay windows with stained glass are all that remain of Macintosh's imprint, however, as the interiors were gutted some time ago. From Balgrayhill the rest of Springburn was, and remains – literally and socially – downhill, though it should be said that in its heyday, Springburn was one of the most prosperous and 'respectable' of Glasgow's working-class areas, because of the high proportion of skilled workers employed in the locomotive works.

Tom Weir wrote something about this respectable working-class world of Springburn, in which he grew up between the wars, in his autobiography, *Weir's World* (1994):

> As a lad I found the noise and stir of Springburn exciting. Each morning an army of locomotive workmen, thousands strong, answered the shriek of the hooters, the noise of their heavy boots clattering on the pavements, all in a uniform of dungarees. Noisy tramcars, bells clanging, would be chuntering up and down Springburn Road, where shops of every kind faced each other, many bearing the logo of Cowlairs Co-operative Society.

Both Tom's parents were from railway working families, and his mother worked as a painter in the locomotive shops for a while after Tom's father died. His was the world of the Boy's Brigade, YMCA, cycling and boxing clubs to keep fit, and trips to Springburn Library or even tramps across Glasgow to the Mitchell Library for self-education. Like many parents at that time, Tom's mother wanted him to have a white-collar job, and on leaving school he started worked in the Co-operative stores. But, not desiring to have engraved on his tombstone 'Born a Man, died a Grocer', Tom eventually managed to escape and earn himself a living as a well-loved broadcaster and writer on the great outdoors, including having a monthly feature in the *Scots Magazine* for many years. One impetus to his outdoor career was that from Springburn's hills you could see the distant, greater hills of the Campsies, and beyond those, Ben Lomond and the mountains of Arrochar.

More than many other areas of Glasgow, Springburn's original street pattern has been obliterated by redevelopment. Dropping down

Balgrayhill along Lenzie Street there is almost nothing left of pre-1960s Springburn. Along Springburn Way some of the former buildings stand, but the centre of Springburn now consists mainly of a shopping centre and a sports centre, which, though functional, are of limited visual interest or architectural merit. Gone are landmarks like Quinn's Bar with its tower clock and its famous (understairs) howff where favoured regulars could drink after hours, immortalised in the song:

> Doon in the wee room underneath the sterr
> Everybody's happy, everybody's there
> Were a' getting merry each in his cherr
> Doon in the wee room underneath the sterr.

Historic Springburn was literally sliced in half in the 1960s by wholescale demolition of good tenement buildings for the construction of the A803 road, the purpose of which was to speed up by a few minutes the daily incoming and exiting of commuters working in Glasgow but living in places like Bishopbriggs – which is not part of Glasgow city, absurdly, though most of its inhabitants work in the city. This road, which so damaged Springburn, was not constructed for its inhabitants, since car ownership there is the Glasgow average of about one-third of households. It forcibly divided one half of Springburn from its shops and facilities by a dual carriageway with associated overpasses, and the demolition for the road has left us – 30 years later – with large vacant grassed-over spaces on each side. One is entitled to ask; why was Glasgow prepared to destroy its own communities for the benefit of rates and, later, community charge tax exiles living outside of the city?

As a symbol of Springburn's neglect, stood for many years the formerly glorious Springburn Public Halls, constructed in 1902. If you looked carefully at the façade on their frontage you could see two Greek goddesses, representing Art and Industry (the latter cradling a locomotive). No more – the Halls were recently demolished as unsafe and unsaveable. Almost the only relic hereabouts of Springburn's glory days is the Co-op Fountain, originally erected in 1902 at the Cross, but moved to the shopping centre in 1981. Its motto is 'Unity is Strength' and it recalls a time when the Co-op was a vital part of working-class life. Indeed, the Springburn and Cowlairs Co-op was largely owned by the local railway workers, and was actually founded in 1881 when workers on strike could not get credit from local shopkeepers. It became a roaring success, with 26 branches.

Another function of the Co-op was to provide a loan for those having to purchase their tools on taking up a railway apprenticeship.

A little further on from the shopping centre you come to Springburn station, whose dilapidated state is a biting irony, given that Springburn was once the world's railway capital. The Hydepark works lay to the south of the railway line, while the Atlas was situated to the north. The latter factory gives its name to Atlas Square, where the Springburn Library was located till recently. A plaque on the wall commemorates the refurbishing of this and the opening of an associated Springburn Museum by Tom Weir in 1988. The library has recently been moved to the sports centre where there is a small display on the history of Springburn, and where the local History Group meets. The library staff are extremely helpful, and the place has a collection of old pictures and maps worth looking at, and leaflets about Springburn's heritage, including one produced for the 1999 Year of Architecture, on Springburn's various historical monuments. There has also recently been published, by Glasgow District Council, a Heritage Trail for Springburn Park. The former library is a now business and workspace unit.

Springburn was an early centre of trades unionism and socialist groupings. In 1890–1 the first national strike of railway men was centred on Springburn, when 9,000 men came out, largely in protest against the enforced working of excessive hours, sometimes up to 20 per day. The Cowlairs and St Rollox works were actually owned by the railway companies, such as the Caledonian Railway, and their workers joined the strike. Gangs of pickets engaged in nocturnal skirmishes with police in the Springburn streets, and the police report of the strike described the incident thus:

> Shortly after midnight a body of strikers, 60-strong, arrived upon the scene, and proceeded in marching order in the direction of the railway at St Rollox. A sufficient number of constables having been brought together, the strikers were charged...

It is significant that the Hydepark works, a family-owned firm, did not join the strike. Reid, its owner, was paternalistic and determinedly anti-union. This attitude at Hydepark continued even after it merged with its rivals to form the North British Locomotive Company, and in the General Strike of 1926, while the other railway workshops came out for the miners, the response at Hydepark was very patchy. (Only in the 1950s, with an influx of militant electricians when the

1891 Rail Strike. A group of workers who engaged in the mass railwaymen's strike of that year in Springburn. How respectable and well-dressed they look! Railway workers, possibly even more than shipyard workers, were the aristocracy of the working class.

works converted to electric trains, did this deferential attitude end at Hydepark.) Generally, though, the 1926 strike was solid in Springburn and J Thomas recalls in *The Springburn Story* that a tramcar driven by a volunteer was hounded out of Springburn by flour bombs – despite the pile of stones lying handy from a demolished building. He comments that, 'The Springburn revolutionaries, rather than throw stones, queued up at the local shop to buy flour bombs at their own expense'. *The Springburn Experience* (1989) by Gerard Hutchison and Mark O'Neill splendidly brings together a wealth of oral history information about working conditions, trades unionism and other aspects of Springburn life.

John Paton was an Aberdonian socialist who came to Glasgow before the First World War to experience what he called 'the more exciting and wider world' of the big city. He got a job in Springburn as a barber and married there, joining the local ILP. He describes the optimism and activity of that period well, and comments in *Proletarian Pilgrimage* (1936):

> The Springburn ILP was a hive of activity. It had about a hundred members and a steady flow of new recruits. For the most part the men belonged to the skilled trades like engineering, and were almost always known as good and steady workmen. They were active trades unionists to a man. The great majority were

total abstainers. There was a strong element of puritanism in their make-up.

Paton's optimism as to the future a century ago – and arrogance about his political correctness – echoes my own on arriving in Glasgow just after the huge industrial struggles of the early 1970s, and thinking that a new world was at hand. Like most other heavily working-class areas of Glasgow, Springburn returned an ILP Red Clydesider member to Westminster in 1922. Paton stood for the ILP in a couple of seats and failed, becoming in turn national organiser and editor of its paper, *New Leader*. Eventually he moved right and became a Labour MP in the 1945 landslide election. His book remains a wonderful account of a historical period, and deserves to be reprinted.

It is surprising and gratifying that anything of Springburn's heritage has escaped the demolition men or the more insidious effects of neglect, but in Flemington Street you can get a glimpse of former glory. The grand buildings here were once the offices of the North British Locomotive Company. Outside are sculptures representing Science and Speed, while over the front door is the splendid carved elevation of a locomotive. But these foretastes are nothing to what lies inside. There are plaques commemorating the dead of both wars who worked for the company, and also the opening of the building by Lord Roseberry in 1908. A magnificent wood and marble staircase leads to the even more magnificent boardroom, which was the teaching staffroom when the building formerly housed the North Glasgow College, now relocated as Kelvin College to a futuristic building on the opposite, north side of Flemington Street. The windows behind the staircase contain striking stained glass First World War memorials, one of which is a fine portrayal of a female munitions worker at her lathe. She looks sad. Maybe she is mourning one of the 300 men from the NBLC killed in action. Whilst it was a college, access was easy and there was even a heritage trail round it, now a polite request may be met with permission – or not. Sadly the building has not yet taken part in the annual Doors Open Day, which would allow assured visitor access.

Glasgow is over-provided with business spaces, like these former NBLC offices. In another part of the city – for example, the West End – a developer would seize upon the opportunity to turn this asset into housing. However, this will not happen in Springburn as long as market forces dominate planning. The cost of converting this building to housing would be so great that the flats would be correspondingly expensive; certainly beyond a price anyone would pay to live in Springburn.

As Springburn Park is the 'dear green place' in the north of the district, so Sighthill Cemetery is the same in the south. Sighthill is so called because of the view that can be had from it, and here in the 1840s Glasgow opened up a large new cemetery. Though not having the status of residents of the Necropolis beside Glasgow Cathedral, where many of Glasgow's *haute bourgeoisie* were buried, those interred in Sighthill were nevertheless 'quality' folk: shipmasters, professional men and the like. James Mossman is buried here, beneath a fairly simple stone. Mossman founded the firm (which still exists near Glasgow Cathedral) of monumental sculptors that was responsible for more public sculpture in Victorian Glasgow than any other. Regrettably, Ray Mackenzie's wonderful book *Sculpture in Glasgow* (1999), which does so much for Mossman's reputation, does not include Mossman's burial stone in it, nor any of the other interesting public sculptures of Springburn. An omission to be corrected, one hopes.

The most famous of those interred at Sighthill were, however, of much lower rank. In 1847, a monument was raised by public subscription to honour John Baird and Andrew Hardie (later James Wilson was also commemorated there). These three men were all executed for taking part in the so-called Radical War of 1820. In that year, the first mass political strike in world history took place when 60,000 workers in the West of Scotland downed tools for the right to vote. Baird, Wilson and Hardie, along with some others, carried their protest as far as armed insurrection, and paid the ultimate price, though their example inspired later generations of reformers who eventually achieved many of the original aims of the men of 1820. (It is often stated that Keir Hardie was a descendant of the 1820 martyr Andrew Hardie, but Hardie was adopted and it was his adoptive brother who was the lineal descendant and who in turn became the ILP member of parliament for Springburn from 1922-37.)

In *Glasgow and its Clubs*, written in 1856, John Strang quotes from the account of a member of the Waterloo Club, a patriotic organisation, describing the panic that seized the city in 1820. The authorities mobilised the soldiers at Bridgeton Barracks and called out volunteer middle-class militias, to defend the city against expected attack. The account states:

From Sunday morning, when the famous or rather infamous inflammatory placard was posted at the corner of the streets, all the public works and factories were closed, while the miners in and around Glasgow struck work.

The volunteer militias patrolled the streets, where 'idle crowds, collected in gloomy groups about the corners of the leading thoroughfares,' and the 'ill-conditioned, irritable and starving working men in Calton, Bridgeton and the Gorbals' were on strike. But only scattered risings took place.

From the cemetery you overlook the housing of Sighthill, now home to many asylum seekers fleeing persecution abroad, and reminding us that even today not everyone has the rights and freedoms for which those like Baird and Hardie fought almost two centuries ago. Sighthill has had its tensions over this asylum issue, but indications now are that community relations are improving. Much of Sighthill's high-rise buildings are already demolished and the area is to be rebuilt with new housing in the style – hopefully – of the New Gorbals. Walking around there made me think of the song 'Freedom Come All Ye' by the late great Scottish writer Hamish Henderson, whose lines cite his hopes for the future:

When John Maclean meets wi his freens in Springburn
A the roses and geans will turn tae bloom
Black and white ane till ither mairreit
Can find bried, barley bree and painted room

We started this exploration of Springburn with the railway 'Emperor' Reid on his hill above Springburn. It is fitting that we end also with a railway theme, and just to the east of Sighthill Park, in the area now occupied by the interstices of the M8 and the A803, stood, till 1964, the St Rollox Chemical Works. With Glasgow, all industrial history is in superlatives – biggest, first, greatest – and St Rollox is no exception. This was the largest chemical works in Europe, as well as one of the oldest, founded in 1797. Its chimney, known as Tennant's Lum, was, at 435 feet, reputedly the highest in the world and a landmark far and wide until it was demolished in 1922. This was also the site of Scotland's first railway, the Garnkirk to Glasgow, which was constructed in 1831 to supply St Rollox with coal, and was opened by none other than George Stephenson, the railway pioneer. St Rollox also created huge chemical waste deposits, which enjoyed an infamy sufficient for Glasgow artist Muirhead Bone to try to convey the sense of desolation they inspired. Today, these wastes lie underneath the housing of Sighthill.

The largest chemical works in the world, like the largest railway workshops, are found no more in Springburn. Belmont mansion is gone, the Winter Gardens are a skeleton, the Public Hall demolished. Like Rome, the streets of Springburn are filled with ruins and ghosts. Springburn's time, like that of Rome, may yet come again. But in the last decade there has been little sign of change here, the building of the new Kelvin College aside. Unlike the Gorbals or Bridgeton, Springburn lies a little too far from booming central Glasgow to benefit from its commercial and housing developments, and it may have to wait a little while for the roses and geans to bloom.

Many districts in Glasgow evoke similar feelings. People were driven here from poverty and oppression in Ireland, from the rest of Scotland, from Russia and elsewhere, and herded into overcrowded housing to work long hard hours for little pay. Yet and yet, they built up a life of community spirit and created organisations of a political, social and religious nature that eventually made their lives tolerable ones. And then the carpet was pulled from under their economic existences, and to that injury was added another injury, as well as an insult, in that their communities were destroyed by reckless planning decisions. Nowhere, but nowhere, is this truer than in Springburn. The much-maligned Red Road flats, now in the process of being demolished, were a blessing to Springburn in comparison to the A803 which literally 'broke Springburn's heart' – as a sculpture on a truncated part of the old Springburn Road to the east of Sighthill Cemetery so eloquently, though wordlessly, conveys. It would have been better to uproot and refill with housing that atrocity of a road, rather than demolish the Red Road flats. How Springburn's broken heart might be mended is not easy to envisage.

CHAPTER TWELVE

Dennistoun: No Mean Streets

THE DISTRICT OF Dennistoun is an island. Not only is it physically situated on rising ground above Townhead, Bridgeton and Parkhead, but it was, and remains to a great extent, socially an island of unflinching respectability in the surrounding East End of Glasgow. For many working-class folk in that part of the town, Dennistoun was the summit of their social ambitions. While socialist activists on Glasgow Green hoped to lead the working classes to the promised land, most of them would just have settled for Dennistoun.

The Glasgow singer Lulu moved to Dennistoun as a girl from Bridgeton, and said in her autobiography *I Don't Want to Fight*:

> When we moved from Soho Street across the railway bridge to Garfield Street, it was only a couple of hundred yards, but mentally it was a lot further. We had edged slightly up in the world because we now lived closer to Duke Street and further away from the Gallowgate. There weren't so many poorly dressed kids or runny noses.

Andrew Stewart dedicated a book of photographs of the area, *Old Dennistoun*, to his parents, who, he says 'had one of their hopes fulfilled when we moved house from Townhead to Dennistoun'. A more famous person whose family moved from Townhead to Dennistoun was Charles Rennie Mackintosh. Like Lulu later, Toshie, whose father was in the police force, had moved a very short distance, but into an area that signified an important step up the social ladder. A mark of its social status and respectability is that until the 1960s, in a city renowned for its alcohol abuse, the Dennistoun area was 'dry'.

But had things developed differently, Dennistoun would not be a by-word for working-class respectability, but instead a residential area for the upper and middle classes to rival Glasgow's West End. Alexander Dennistoun was from a Glasgow banking family, and in 1856 he engaged the renowned architect James Salmon to plan and lay out a residential suburb called after him. Only a few streets were built in the 1850s and 1860s, before the spread of the heavy industries roundabout caused the plan to be aborted. Tucked away between Duke Street and Alexandra Parade, the villas and terraces that remain from Salmon's Grand Design are one of the little-known treasures of Glasgow. In 1872, John Tweed's *Guide to Glasgow and the Clyde* had this area very definitely on the tourist itinerary, recommending a walk to 'the pleasant suburb of Dennistoun. It is well laid out and contains many fine villas and lodges. The approach by Alexandra Parade is very fine'. The area was subsequently feued for the building of tenements from the 1870s, although they were of a quality generally much higher than the rest of the East End. These 'less ornamental houses for artisans' had by 1914 made Dennistoun the residential location of the aristocracy of the working class.

And Dennistoun had had another false start before finding its identity, being the location of one of the birthplaces of the Industrial Revolution. In the 1770s George Macintosh, in partnership with David Dale of New Lanark, established a factory in Dennistoun to the east of the present Necropolis. This was set up to produce cudbear, a dye for the textile industry. As well as the factory, Macintosh built a model village for his workers, with housing and educational facilities. The roll call at the Dunchattan works every morning was in Gaelic, for Macintosh employed only Gaelic speakers. The reason for this was not that the Highlanders had a good reputation as hard workers (on the contrary) but that being Gaelic speakers, and being discouraged from communicating with people from outwith the settlement (he even surrounded the factory with a high wall), Macintosh hoped to be able to protect his industrial secrets from competitors.

George's son Charles continued the business and experimented in industrial chemistry, having taken classes with Joseph Black at Glasgow University. He discovered that ammonia, in the form of naphtha, a by-product to the making of his cudbear, would dissolve rubber. This gave birth to the waterproofing of textiles, and the dubbing of such garments as 'macintoshes'. Shortly before his death in 1843, Macintosh moved the works to Manchester and Dennistoun's contribution to industrial progress ceased, for it never again became a centre of industry. This period is, however, commemorated in the naming of the 1970s and '80s housing developments located at Dunchattan Street and Macintosh Court on the site of the former works.

After this experiment ended, people tended to live in Dennistoun, but not to work in it. For, unlike many of the other areas of Glasgow where housing and manufacturing were in close proximity (but however in this respect like Govanhill) industry was located at the

Dennistoun

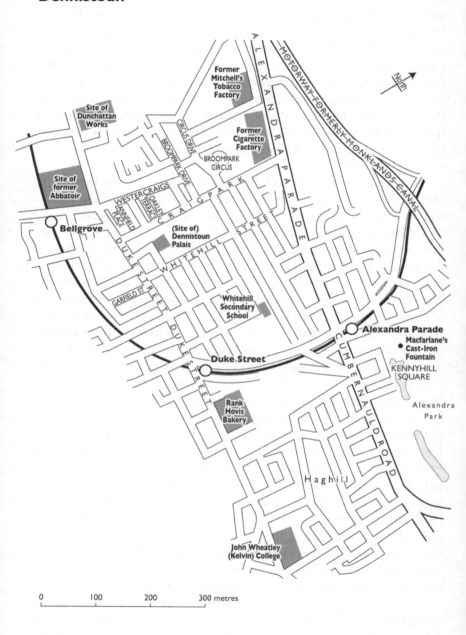

Dennistoun Route Summary

1   Alight at Bellrove station, then take a right across Duke Street.

2   Walk up Westercraigs to Broompark Circus (Highfield) and Circus Drive.

3   Continue along the entire length of Alexandra Parade, then enter Alexandra Park (Macfarlane Fountain).

4   When you reach Kennyhill Square, cross the Parade to wander through Haghill at leisure, and arrive at the Wheatley (Kelvin) College.

5   Go back along Duke Street and past the Rank Hovis bakery to re-enter Dennistoun proper.

6   Meander through the fine grid-plan tenement-lined streets before stopping for refreshments at Tapa, Tibo or Coia's, all clustered on, or just off, western Duke Street.

7   Return to Bellgrove railway station.

Approximate route time: 3 hours

edges of Dennistoun. To the east lay the chemical works, to the south-west the slaughterhouse, and to the north the Blochairn steelworks and Provanmill gasworks, the latter separated from Dennistoun by the Monklands Canal. All these were firmly outwith the residential streets of the area. Later, Alexandra Parade became the centre of Glasgow's cigarette industry and was awarded the name Tobacco Road. But even there, you were past the factories before you arrived at the tenement buildings. With its lack of industry and its good housing, it is easy to understand why so many in Calton or Camlachie looked enviously uphill at the denizens of Dennistoun.

Dennistoun's position as the area's jewel in the crown was recog-nised when it was chosen to stage both the East End Industrial Exhi-bitions; that of 1890–91 and the subsequent one in 1903–4; 750,000 attended the first and over a million the second. The first raised £3,000 for the building of the People's Palace, which many expected would be in Dennistoun's Alexandra Park, but was instead placed on Glasgow Green. The educational exhibits drew crowds, but the main event was the 'Buffalo Bill' Wild West Show, starring Colonel William F Cody himself, as well as Annie Oakley. Dennistoun was later to produce many characters in the world of entertainment to rival Buffalo Bill. But so far only Bill has his statue, a small one of him on a bucking bronco in a wee garden located in a new housing development off Roslea Drive.

Which brings us back to Lulu. Let us start, as she did, with a railway crossing. The train today deposits the traveller at Bellgrove station and on exiting, to the left is towards Bridgeton, literally on the wrong side of the tracks. To the right, across the railway bridge Lulu saw as a social marker, is Dennistoun. On crossing Duke Street and heading up Westercraigs, you are in the heart of what was actually executed of Salmon's plans for a grand suburb. Salmon himself originally lived here, at 7 Broompark Drive, and so too did Sir William Arrol, who opened his Dalmarnock Iron Works in Bridgeton in 1868, and who is best remembered for the construction of the Forth Railway Bridge in 1890. Arrol gave 10 Oakley Terrace, Dennistoun, as his main address in the Post Office street directory from 1880 until he moved in his '60s to Seafield in Ayr in 1901. It should be remembered that in the 1860s the University was still on the nearby High Street, less than a mile away; its move westwards was another blow to Salmon's great plans.

At the bottom of Westercraigs is Annfield Place, terraced houses formerly occupied by lawyers, doctors and engineers – and now the location of the offices of the same professions, since such people don't now live in Dennistoun, respectable though it is. Once off Duke Street the terraces replicate themselves and are still quality housing, with the larger villas lying just to the westward. At the top of the hill is the delightful Broompark Circus. Hereabouts it is really hard to believe that you are in Glasgow's East End, with its collection of fine villas in their grounds. Most notable is Highfield, sadly unoccupied and boarded up since the council stopped using it as a nursery. Just north of this area were the tobacco factories, and much of the land abandoned by them is being developed for modern quality housing. Gentrification is nibbling at the edges of Dennistoun; indeed, it is biting off chunks of the area.

Glasgow's connection with tobacco goes back to the 18th century and the tobacco lords, who made their wealth from the trade in the weed with the American colonies. The cigarette industry was a much later development, making the fortunes of men such as Stephen Mitchell, whose legacy endowed the Mitchell Library in the city. One of his factories was located at Alexandra Parade, and is now refurbished as a collection of studios, The Wasps Factory, for arts workers. Next to it stands the Wills' factory, an imposing, though rather late, example of Art Deco completed in the early 1950s. This, too, has ceased cigarette production and was refurbished as a business centre for high-tech and advertising firms. Today, Glasgow's only connection with tobacco sadly lies in the continued high consumption by its citizens of cigarettes and the consequent high mortality rates.

Alexandra Parade is a pleasant street of solid tenements, with neat gardens on the north side and neat shops on the south, which leads to Alexandra Park. Outside is found a good example of Glasgow ironwork, a Macfarlane fountain beside the park gates. But if this impresses, you are in for a greater delight. Inside the park can be found another fountain, possibly the finest example of the work of the Saracen Iron Foundry still to be seen in Glasgow. Walter Macfarlane built this at Possil, and exhibited it at the 1901 Empire Exhibition; thereafter it was relocated to the park, and it has recently been restored. The classical female figures represent Art, Literature, Science and Commerce. I was taking some photographs and got into conversation, as is often unavoidable in Glasgow. A local, obviously proud of the fountain, told me that there used to be fish in it, and that as a kid he would come and catch them.

'It's disgraceful,' he added. 'There should still be fish in it.'

'Maybe if you hadn't kept catching them, there still would be?' I suggested.

Alexandra Park was opened in 1870 and was supposed to be the East End equivalent of the West End's Kelvingrove: a polite watering place. The westward flight of the middle classes has left the folk of Dennistoun with a huge area for recreation and a very fine park, hosting a municipal golf course. Formerly, the inhabitants, and especially the weans, had more exciting attractions. Before the motorway, the Monklands Canal separated Dennistoun from the city to the north, and the canal banks were a favourite recreational spot, especially the waterfall at Riddrie Locks, which flowed once the locks became derelict. Further on at Riddrie Knowes were the Sugerolly Mountains, multicoloured chemical deposits where the kids would go sledging in winter, doubtless at great but unknown threats to their health.

Just after the park gates lies the former United Free Church built in 1904, whose hall was designed by James Salmon II, grandson of the original Dennistoun planner. Salmon didn't get the contract for the church, to his chagrin, but history has turned his hall into the modern

church, while the church itself has been converted into flats. A fine
Faith, Hope and Love motif crowns the building. Just further on
Kennyhill Square, with its neat bowling green, is the acme of Dennistoun respectability, with trim tenements and wally closes, the exteriors
of which actually have granite pillars on the door entrances. Jack
House was brought up here, and describes his boyhood in *Pavement
in the Sun* (1967).

Past Kennyhill Square, on the south side of The Parade, you come
to Haghill, an area built later than the Parade and of poorer tenemented housing; here you feel you are struggling to keep your feet
above the waters of the East End. Jack House went to Haghill primary
school where one of his teachers was James Maxton. This imposing
school and its fine janitor's house are currently boarded up and decaying. The northern part of Haghill does not have the air of prosperity
that Dennistoun 'proper' has, and southwards are cleared areas where
poor quality social housing built in the 1930s as slum clearance, has
itself been demolished without anything taking its place. This feeling
of being in a different world is confirmed as you walk south down
Cumbernauld Road towards Duke Street station and overlook the
lands towards Parkhead, once occupied by a long-gone chemical
works to the south of Duke Street, and to the north of it by the still
functioning Rank Hovis Bakery. A pub unashamedly proclaiming its
sectarian footballing allegiance and a criminal lawyer's office reveals
that even douce Dennistoun has its underbelly. I stopped to take a
photo of the quaint mural of a criminal behind bars, which formerly
graced the lawyer's window. Out of the aforementioned pub staggered
a punter, who watched me curiously, then stated, 'He'll no get ye aff'.

I asked for an explanation and found out that my new friend
thought I was in need of legal aid, in relation to some unspecified
offence, and recommended another practitioner to me.

'He gets ivverybody aff,' I was assured, and noted the fact for
future use.

From Duke Street station, Duke Street, the longest in Britain,
stretches away east towards Parkhead. Staying on the Dennistoun side
of the railway it is one world but a few yards along on the opposite it
is another. There are no waste plots in Dennistoun, but as you head
east along Duke Street towards Parkhead you enter the third world
of abandoned rubbish, waste ground occupied by dookits and boarded-up or burnt-out housing, all of which characterise the lower end
of Haghill. The outstanding exception is the former John Wheatley

College, now run under the Kelvin College umbrella, a veritable oasis for the eye. South of Duke Street is a warren of abandoned factories and some still-functioning small workshops, as well as a large site for travelling (shows) people. You can understand the desperation with which the respectable working classes sought to differentiate themselves from the underclass. To this day, the sternest critics of the lumpen proletariat are the better-off working classes.

Nevertheless, though estate agents and property developers will try to make it otherwise, the sense of Haghill as being part of Dennistoun is deeply rooted. Impressionistic evidence can be gained by simply asking people in the street, but I undertook a more scientific sampling at a talk I gave in Dennistoun Library, attended by a healthy audience of 30. Whilst agreeing that Haghill wasn't as respectable or prosperous, only one person insisted it was not actually Dennistoun – and he was from Haghill!

Heading back along Duke Street, this underworld is left behind and we are again passing through well-maintained shops and tenements. On or off Duke Street are also several excellent eateries, like the Coia Café of 1922 – but updated to modern eating – the Tibo gastro hub and the excellent vegetarian wholefood joint, Tapa. For Dennistoun flats are now seem as desirable by middle-class purchasers, pushing up their prices, and new private housing has also been erected, for example on the site of the old Dennistoun Palais and of a former school on Roslea Drive and Whitehill Street. But at the same time, there is the proliferation here of the sight of pawnbrokers and money lenders' shops, as well as charity shops sitting cheek by jowl with not-inexpensive clothes shops. Dennistoun is not only being gentrified, it is being polarised. Rising house prices, higher rents and shops selling more expensive quality items do not benefit everyone. They are of negative benefit if you are poor.

Whitehill Street was once the home of another famous Glasgow entertainer, Dorothy Paul, whose *Dorothy: Revelations of a Rejected Soprano* (2002) describes Dennistoun in the 1940s and '50s. This warm and amusing book tells of a mid-20th century working-class upbringing and life with sympathy and a lack of the sentimentalism so often an aspect of Glasgow *sterrheid* writing.

Dorothy went to Whitehill School in Dennistoun, which, before comprehensive education, was the non-denominational senior secondary for a large part of Glasgow's East End. It is therefore unsurprising that it was the nursery of much popular talent, especially in the fields of entertainment and culture. Dorothy admits in her autobiography that she was not a model pupil, and her irreverent attitude to her teachers probably didn't help:

> We were waiting for the teacher to arrive when who should walk in the door but Tojo the Japanese war criminal. I thought he had been hanged, but no, he was a maths teacher in Whitehill Senior Secondary.

> Our (history) teacher was a ringer for John Christie the mass murderer. He drooled over blood and gore, and later 'found God'. He ended going around the streets of Glasgow making a cult of himself.

Dorothy's career has had its ups and downs, and when after a difficult period she had re-established herself, she returned to Whitehill to pioneer her first one-woman show for the staff and pupils. I was fortunate enough to teach Dorothy history at Clydebank College, where she was an outstanding mature student, and was doubly fortunate to be invited to this performance. I was triply fortunate in that the comments on my teaching abilities in her book are thankfully less critical than those on her Whitehill history teacher!

Aside from Dorothy, the school also produced Lulu, Rikki Fulton, the film and TV actor Bill Patterson, Jack House, Adam McNaughton, composer of modern-day street songs, and Alasdair Gray, author of *Lanark* who is considered by many to be Scotland's greatest living writer. Quite a crop.

Dennistoun denizens have produced many autobiographies, and I have referred to some. (In fact they have produced more than any other area of the city, far ahead of Govan and Gorbals, poor seconds.) Common themes emerge from perusing these. Most Dennistounians were the offspring of skilled or white-collar workers. Dorothy's dad was an electrician, Jack House's a steelwork's clerk and Rikki Fulton's was a locksmith (he first worked in Singers in Clydebank but later opened his own shop). Most also appear to have had 'kirkie' upbringings – the Boys' Brigade, the Church Choir and so on. Apart from the inevitable involvement in the Co-operative Society, few in Dennistoun appear to have had serious political leanings in an otherwise political city. Their lives were a far cry from the standard visions of Glasgow working-class life – or mostly they were.

Once the Carnegie Library, yet another fine JR Rhind library built in 1905–6 (look up for the angel on the cupola!) appears on your right, and just off Duke Street you are back near your starting place, with Salmon's villas and terraces on that right side, and the tenements on your left. Here in Garfield Street was where Lulu lived, but her experience of Dennistoun was not happy – or typical. A little further on lie the vacant spaces of the long-demolished Glasgow Corporation abattoir where her father worked; symbolically, it straddles the railway line between Dennistoun and Bridgeton/Calton. For Lulu's dad was a drunkard and a wife-beater, as she makes clear in her autobiography. He was also a part of the East End semi-criminal underworld, regularly stealing quantities of meat from the abattoir and selling them to local butchers.

The song 'Cod Liver Oil and the Orange Juice' describes an unsavoury character at the Dennistoun Palais; he gets obscenely drunk and then behaves badly to a young lady. The song emphasises that he was *not* from Dennistoun:

> Oot o the east there came a hard man
> Oh, ho aa the wye fae Brigton.

The Palais circa 1950s: This new palais opened in 1938, replacing the old one from the '20s that was destroyed by a fire. Dancing and cinema were the two main poles of male and female working-class entertainment between 1920 and 1960, encompassing both the sexes.

Went intae a pub, came oot paralytic
Oh, ho VP and cider, a helluva mixture.

I feel sure that the inhabitants of Dennistoun would have looked disapprovingly at Lulu's dad and ascribed his bad behaviour to his Bridgeton origins. They might have ascribed their own avoidance of such a fate to their good fortune in being raised in an area, which, above all, valued and epitomised working-class respectability.

For the vast majority of working people, even in 'political' Glasgow, life was the pursuit of the calculus of differential advantage. The search was for a better job, for a better house in a better area, or betterment abroad. Apart from a minority who were politically engaged and committed, the mass of working people sought improvement or escape in entertainment, in sport as a career or as a supporter, or in taking to the hills and mountains. Unions, the Labour Party and, for a while, the Co-ops, offered social solidarity for working people, but also, importantly, career outlets for a minority of them. These political activities, or even joining the masons or the Kirk, or the Orange Lodge, were forms of this hoped-for incremental advantage. (In the slums and ghettoes, these aspirations were replaced by crime.) Dennistoun epitomises this search for improvement.

No Mean Streets rather than No Mean City, that's Dennistoun.

CHAPTER THIRTEEN

Parkhead: Paradise Lost

TO SOME, THE name Parkhead may conjure up Paradise, though in truth the district does not really start until one has gone beyond the east side of the stadium of Celtic FC. The western side of Paradise lies in a sub-division of Bridgeton. Parkhead has the same rich heavy industrial past as its westerly neighbour, but without Bridgeton's manifold pre-industrial references, and possibly with a more problematic future.

The first known mention of Parkhead dates from 1794 when there was an inn of that name at the junction of the Tollcross Road and the Gallowgate. Six years after there was a post office at Parkhead, and round about were opened a series of coal mines and engineering works. With the surrounding weavers' settlements, the population of the area was still only around 2,000. A century later, Parkhead and its satellites (including Tollcross) had a population of 50,000, a growth down to the development of the iron and steel industry and in particular to Parkhead Forge. David Willox wrote his *Memoirs of Parkhead* in the 1920s, describing the district from the 1850s onwards, when

Beardmore's Works circa 1950s: An image of the works when Parkhead Forge – and Parkhead – were in deep decline from former greatness. Once employing 15,000 men, the works was finally closed in the '80s and was demolished.
Image courtesy of John Hume

Parkhead

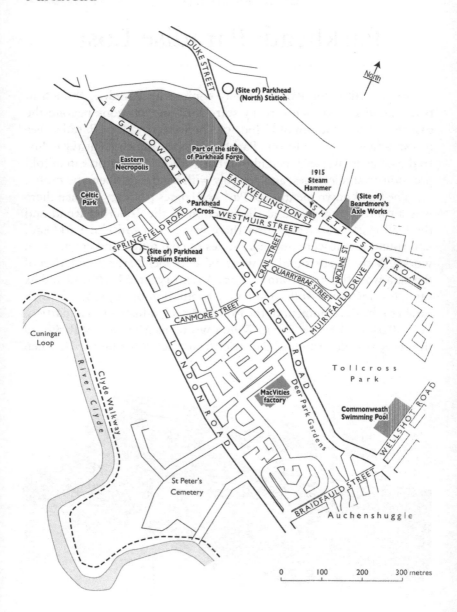

Parkhead Route Summary

1   Like Possil, Parkhead is an area not well-served by public transport. To begin, get to the bottom of Springfield Road (where there once was a station), and walk up to Parkhead Cross and its fine cluster of buildings. (The Eastern Necropolis is worth a diversion.)

2   Proceed down Westmuir Street and cross over to see the 1915 Steam Hammer.

3   Turn up Caroline Street and enter Tollcross Park (with the possibility of refreshments in the Winter Gardens) at Muiryfauld Drive, and follow the delightful route down the Tollcross Burn to Tollcross Road and Deer Park Gardens.

4   Proceed west till you come to Canmore Street and follow this road down to the London Road.

5   Head further back east along the London Road, then at St Peter's Cemetery gain the Clyde Walkway and head westwards, opposite the Cuningar Loop, until you can exit to Springfield Road.

Approximate route time: 3 hours

it was still a collection of industrial villages in a semi-rural setting. The tenements appeared from the 1880s. Parkhead, with its neighbours of Tollcross and Shettleston, still retains several examples of the pre-tenement style of cottage housing, largely disappeared elsewhere from Glasgow's streets. Whitelaw's pub in Tollcross Road near Parkhead Cross, for example, retains the look of a pre-industrial weaver's cottage, though much remodeled.

The focus of the community was and is the present Cross of Parkhead. Its original name was the Sheddens, from an Anglo-Saxon word meaning 'the parting of the ways'. Some older people still know it by this name, which is very appropriate, since the junction is in the form of a K, rather than a proper Cross. The buildings around Parkhead Cross reflect the area's glory days. The Glasgow Savings Bank, designed by architect John Keppie, is the finest building in Parkhead, with its embossed lettering and sculpted figures. The solid sandstone tenements at the gushet of the K-junction also tell of when this was a vibrant, growing and prosperous community, as do JR Rhind's Carnegie Library and the Co-operative building, in the adjacent Tollcross Road

and Westmuir Street respectively. But a short walk in any direction
from the Kross shows that these glory days, and most of the buildings,
workplaces and people associated with them, are long gone. Paradise
Lost here.

The stadium remains, however, despite past plans to move to an
outer-city site. Celtic came here in 1888, after being founded by
Brother Walfrid. The ostensible aim of the club was to help the poor
and needy, and doubtless it did. But the creation of Celtic FC also was
an expression of the desire of the Catholic clergy to keep their faithful
from supporting other teams where they might mix with the unfaith-
ful. To this day, the Catholic clergy have free entry to Paradise – or at
least to Celtic Park. Of great influence there, their influence on the
Labour movement was disproportionate and negative. A study of
Scottish Labour leaders in the 20th century showed that over 50 per
cent were secularists or atheists. Of the remaining religiously inclined
half, only 14 per cent were Catholics, roughly their representation in
the population at large. Yet, because in key areas the clergy could have
a large influence on how working-class Catholics voted, and these
votes could turn otherwise finely balanced elections, Catholic views
became difficult to challenge. The Red Clydesiders, for example,
stayed silent on segregated schooling and on birth control issues; even
Maxton, to his discredit.

Duke Street, reputedly Britain's longest, starts in central Glasgow
and ends at Parkhead Cross. It still leads to Parkhead Forge. Not to
the steel foundry, but to the present widely scattered shopping centre
that took over the name of the industrial undertaking. Though much
of the work is part-time and casual, the new Forge employs almost as
many people as the old one did in its peace-time glory. Most of the
work is unskilled, and much of it is low paid. People welcome the jobs,
though many of the local shops have been killed off, and the banks
and similar facilities have moved into The Forge. It is also better to
see a brown site used for such a development rather than another
out-of-town blight being built at some motorway interchange. When
you look at this shopping complex, you realise how vast Parkhead
Forge was, for much of the space left by its final closure in 1981 is still
awaiting development. Apart from its huge wall along the south side
of Shettleston Road, there is nothing left of the forge. The fine steam
hammer which adorns the Westmuir Street/Wellington Street gushet is
Glasgow-built, but was was not actually used in Parkhead Forge. And
the remaining building at No 179 on the north side of the road, now

housing a revivalist church, was not – as often stated – a Beardmore office block, but a Labour exchange constructed in the mass unemployment of the 1930s.

The forge at Parkhead was founded in 1837 by the Reoch brothers, beginning modestly, like many others at that time, by forging iron from scrap. It was taken over by David Napier, who expanded it to produce steel for the growing shipbuilding industry and was then sold to a partnership, including William Beardmore Senior in 1863. Already Parkhead's biggest employer with 700 workers, Beardmore expanded the forge still further, installing the world's biggest lathe to turn propeller shafts for shipbuilding. When William Beardmore Junior took over in 1879, he replaced the 100-ton steam hammer *Samson* with the 500-ton *Goliath*, again the biggest in the world in its time. He also installed the more efficient Siemens open hearth furnaces at the plant, which were probably the most advanced of their kind in the world around 1900.

Parkhead Forge produced not only steel forgings for ships, but also for construction work, and supplied William Arrol of Bridgeton with 20,000 tons of cast steel for the building of Tower Bridge in London. Covering 18 hectares, the works employed 5,000 men in their peace-time days before 1914, but even then much of their work was for the expanding arms race. In 1905 Beardmore's built the 110 feet high gun-quenching tower for casting artillery, atop the existing building. At the time, this made Parkhead Forge the highest building in Scotland, and it was dubbed 'Parkhead Cathedral'. The tower was demolished in 1969 as the works contracted.

Beardmore's dominated life in Parkhead. Almost every family had someone who worked in the Forge and the firm owned many other ancillary works nearby, such as the crane works and the wheel and axle works, both in Rigby Street, as well as a commercial motor factory in the appropriately named Van Street. Furthermore, Beardmore bought an entire steelworks at Mossend to ensure quality in his steel supplies and also laid out a new shipyard in Dalmuir to build ships himself. Before the First World War he was Scotland's largest employer and the firms directly or partly controlled by him employed almost 100,000 workers.

The furnaces of the forge burned night and day, brightening the Parkhead sky, and the reverberation of the hammers created a constant noise. Tom Bell, an early Parkhead socialist, recalled in his book *Pioneering Days* (1941) that in the 1880s 'the smell of oil and smoke, the thud of the *Samson* hammer and the glare of the furnaces were fast banishing the sights and sounds and colours of the country'. Another Beardmore socialist, Davie Kirkwood, remembered that when the *Goliath* hammer was installed and in operation, 'the whole district quivered as in an earthquake'.

William Beardmore was nothing if not ambitious. He helped finance some of Shackleton's polar explorations and had the Beardmore Glacier named after him (Shackleton repaid Beardmore by having an affair with his wife). But he overreached, and was verging on bankruptcy when he was forced to amalgamate with Vickers in 1902 and make the company a limited one, ending total family control. The First World War gave him breathing space. Parkhead employed 20,000 people working 24 hours a day producing munitions. Beardmore was nicknamed the Field Marshall of Industry and knighted as Lord Invernairn.

After the war, at a time of economic depression, he tried to expand into new areas like aircraft building and motor car production, but the firm was effectively bankrupt and the banks took over in the mid-1920s, forcing Sir William into an early retirement. He died in 1936, before which many of his schemes had crashed and much of his empire had been dismantled. The forge carried on, boosted again by war in 1939 and reconstruction afterwards, but on an ever-reducing scale as shipbuilding contracted.

On Parkhead Forge were centred many of the events of the period of Red Clydeside a century ago. Davie Kirkwood was convenor of shop stewards at Beardmore's and provided his account of those times in his book *My Life of Revolt* (1935). The fact that this had a preface by Winston Churchill showed that Kirkwood mellowed with time. Elected to Parliament in 1922 for the ILP, he eventually moved to Labour. He was knighted, spending his comfortable retirement in Bearsden, far from Parkhead, with the odd trip to the House of Lords.

Kirkwood was criticised by many for his cosy relationship with Beardmore, for succumbing to the discreet charm of the bourgeoisie, and during the Dilution Crisis of 1915 he played a Judas role, and broke the struggle of the Clyde Workers' Committee by doing a separate deal at Parkhead Forge to introduce dilution and boost war production, in return for concessions to the unions. John Maclean attacked Kirkwood and others of the CWC for not opposing the war, but simply using it as a means to get improvements from the employers on trades union issues. There is a road that leads to the House of

Lords, and one to a pauper's grave; Kirkwood took the former, and John Maclean the latter. It is possible that Kirkwood has gone to rest in a place where the fires are hotter than those of Parkhead Forge.

Walking along Shettleston Road gives you an idea of the scale of the old forge. Actor John Cairney was born in Parkhead and he recalled in *East End to West End* (1988) a trip along Shettleston Road that broadened his horizons. In the 1930s Parkhead kids used to jump onto lorries to hitch lifts, then hop off at traffic lights. But one driver became so annoyed at this practice that he drove through all the red lights till he got out of Glasgow. When the lorry stopped a terrified Cairney was deposited on the pavement:

> But as I looked up I saw a castle and I was absolutely stunned. What a sight it was: Edinburgh Castle. It was a fantastic wonder-land to a Glasgow keelie.

Westmuir Street is a pleasant street to amble along, and on the right is the Eastern Co-op Building of 1903, which in turn has a plaque commemorating the Parkhead and Westmuir Economical Society of 1831, the area's first Co-op. A cut along Crail Street takes you to Quarrybrae Street and an interesting building. This looks like a school, and though it functioned as a further education college annex for a while, it was actually built a century ago as a Model Lodging House for the multitudes of unskilled workers who flocked here to work. A building workers' strike in Parkhead was broken at that time by bringing in Irish labour to complete the work. Many strikebreakers stayed at the Model and old Parkhead folk used to call this Scabby Loan in remembrance.

Few Glasgow working-class areas do not have enclaves of superior dwellings; in the days when people had to live close to their work, housing for clerical and professional and managerial workers within distance of employment was necessary. The greatest surprise in this area is the trio of streets bordering Tollcross Park – just up Quarrybrae from the old Model, too. The southern part, Muiryfauld Drive, is a line of solid semi-detached villas overlooking the park, and Tennyson Drive and Drumover Drive are scarcely less fine. Dropping downhill to Caroline Street and those roads around it, and you are back in working-class Parkhead, one where there are many derelict areas of cleared housing, though a start has been made on new build. Amazingly, there is still a small functioning factory here: Twinning's Twine factory, heavily fortified.

Tollcross Park is a Glasgow success story and its restoration is a wonderful boon to the people of Parkhead and other areas adjoining it. The lands here were owned by the Dunlop family. The Dunlops had been amongst the city's leading tobacco lords, but moved out of that trade and into the coming thing – coal and iron. They sank many coal pits in Tollcross, but they wanted the fuel mainly to smelt iron, and in the early 1800s established the Clyde Iron Works at Tollcross. They were lucky enough to allow a Shettleston man, John Nielson, to try his new-fangled hot blast in their furnaces, allowing a great reduction in fuel costs and improvement of the quality of iron. The family prospered as never before, and Colin Dunlop became Glasgow's first post-Reform Act MP in 1835. The family mansion was built in the grounds of Tollcross by James Bryce in the 1840s, in Scots Baronial style. The Dunlops suffered in the depression of the 1870s, with falling iron prices and the emergence of trades unionism in their workforce, and a series of strikes followed as they tried to cut wages. Steel, not iron, was now the new idea, and by the 1890s the Dunlops were bankrupt, selling the park to Glasgow Council for £30,000 (about £3 million today).

The mansion became a children's museum, then became derelict, as too did the Winter Gardens. Lottery money restored the latter in 1996, and locals successfully combatted plans to sell the mansion as luxury flats. Instead it was converted to sheltered housing for elderly people and is presently run by an offshoot arm of the Church of Scotland. The park has designated walks and a children's farm within its boundaries, and is excellently maintained and well used. Also, a new swimming pool was built in a former area of the park, for the 2014 Commonwealth Games. The Tollcross model is one that Springburn Park, mentioned in Chapter 11, should be allowed to follow.

On the south side of the park is what was probably the finest set of tenements in the whole East End, on a section of Tollcross Road known as Deer Park Gardens, giving a marvelous architectural line up the brae towards Parkhead proper. Behind it is the McVities biscuit factory, still employing about 500 people and the largest of the few industrial units left in Parkhead. Deer Park Gardens gives an interesting insight into the Property Owning Democracy and its discontents. Almost all of these houses are privately owned, yet in the years I have been passing them there has been an undeniable decline, albeit slow, in their fabric. Clearly, people might afford the houses but then the insurance and repair costs can be prohibitive. It has been estimated that 50 per cent of the privately owned housing stock in Glasgow is in serious need of repair. Yet a little further west along Tollcross Road is a slightly less splendid line of tenements, equally long, which was upgraded some time back by the local housing association; the quality of repair of these buildings is higher than that of Deer Park Gardens. The housing policies of the last 30 years have forced many people into the property market who struggle to be there, and their inability to maintain their properties leads to the creation of the slums of the future.

Parkhead is one of the few areas of Glasgow without a railway. Formerly it had two: Parkhead North, handy for the forge and Parkhead Stadium, handy for the fitba'. Both were closed by the early 1960s. Ideas were floated about re-opening these for the 2014 Commonwealth Games, but funds were used to build a new link road slicing through Dalmarnock instead. The area used to be well-served by trams, however, and the last one in 1962 ran to the famous satellite of Parkhead known as Auchenshuggle. This event produced its usual Glasgow ditty, a variation on the 'Last Train to San Fernando' lyric:

> Last tram tae Auchenshuggle, Last tram tae Auchenshuggle
> If you miss this one you'll never get another one
> Biddy biddy bum bum tae Auchenshuggle.

Auchenshuggle is no joke, as you will notice going down Braidfauld Street. The shops here, such as Honest Joe's, which advertises 'Tic for the needy', are a mocking counterpoint to the gloss of the new Forge. At Potter Street, off the London Road, were found the Govancroft Potteries, another Glasgow pottery whose wares are now collectible, since it closed in the late 1980s. On the opposite side of London Road to Potter Street is St Peter's Cemetery, and a lane leads past the cemetery. Take the lane, braving the rubbish, and you come to the banks of the Clyde at one of its most delightful spots, which seems a million miles away from Auchenshuggle.

Here the river takes a series of vast loops between the city and Rutherglen and Cambuslang on the opposite bank. They are called the Cuningar Loops, after an old Scots name for a rabbit, which infested the area. Even when this region was dominated by heavy industry, much of it was undeveloped. In the 1930s James Cowan, in *From Glasgow's Treasure Chest*, recorded the wonder he felt when he saw 'in a wide flat valley more than forty horses grazing... and fields of cabbage, corn and potatoes filling up most of the land enclosed by the river'. Now much of the industrial waste has been grown over and the site abounds with flora and fauna of every description. A £5 million scheme between the Forestry Commission and Clyde Gateway will transform the Loop into an urban parkland, with a footbridge connection to the Dalmarnock side of the river, by 2015. But that wasn't Plan A. The original idea of Oor City Faithers was instead to cover the area with an extension of the motorway system and to put all the bends of the Clyde into an underground pipe. I didn't make that up, honest. You couldn't. Work on the M74 extension has now been completed in this area but takes a different route into the city, south of the River Clyde.

As well as the delights of the river, here by the Clyde's banks you will find a strange wall that crosses the path. Till the end of the 19th century this was known as Harvie's Dyke, and its tale is worth telling. Around 1800, Parkhead was a collection of mining and weaving hamlets, whose inhabitants regularly fought each other as a form of entertainment. However, faced with a common danger they could unite, and the colliers, weavers and others of Parkhead joined with those of Carmyle and Dalmarnock in defence of their traditional rights of access to the Clyde. In 1819 Thomas Harvie, a local distiller, acquired the lands of Westhorn and built a dyke at both ends of his property right down into the river to prevent pedestrian access to the banks. In July 1822, a large mob demolished the dyke with picks and crowbars. The Enniskillen Dragoons were called out, shots were fired, and the leaders of the protest arrested and imprisoned. A fund was raised for their defence, the case went to the House of Lords, Harvie was defeated and the men released. Harvie disappeared to Ireland after some shady financial dealings, but so too did the £384 surplus of the fund raised for the men's defence. A medal was struck to commemorate the deed in 1829.

This was just one aspect of the radicalism of Parkhead. In 1820, many of the weavers and colliers had struck in the fight for parliamentary reform, in the so-called Radical War. It is argued by some that the address calling for strike action and reform was actually drawn up in Parkhead itself. The area was also a stronghold of Chartism in the 1840s. Some of the first Co-operatives were founded in Parkhead, the earliest being the Parkhead and Westmuir Economical Society in 1831. In 1839 a Scientific Association was opened with a library of almost 1,000 books, sustained by local working men. The militancy around the time of the First World War had solid roots in Parkhead's past.

Negotiating your way along the river behind the former Belvidere

Hospital you re-emerge into post-industrial Parkhead at the junction of London Road and Springfield Road. In the old days, it was the Forge's quenching tower that was visible from everywhere in Parkhead; now it is the cantilevers of Celtic Park. Springfield Road used to be known as Dry Thrapple Lane, from the stour raised before it was paved and before Glasgow people lost much of their Scots dialect. To the south is the new Commonwealth Games Village, to be discussed under Bridgeton, but there is much to see on the way back to the Cross, where we are returning. A fine tenement stands on the left of the street, whilst a group of 1960s medium-rise blocks have been very well restored on the right, and new housing is gradually filling the gaps elsewhere.

If your thrapple was dry in the old days, you no doubt repaired to the Black Bull Inn in the Gallowgate, just west of Parkhead Cross. This building dated from 1760 and was reputed to be the oldest in the whole area. It is commemorated in a poem by John Breckenridge, celebrating the opening of a baker's establishment near to the pub:

> It's auld Ne'er day an! We're met i' the 'Bull'
> Wi oor hearts dancin' licht, an' a bowl flowing full
> Let envy and spite throw aff a' disguise
> And drink to young Gibbie that's gi'en us the pies.

A pie and a pint have a long pedigree in Parkhead. There is still a Black Bull here, but not the original one, as the current pub is situated in a tenement built in 1902.

The owner of the Black Bull also produced his own light beverages, but was bought out by a Falkirk man, JK Barr, in the 1880s. Barr's successors in the family produced a drink called Iron-Brew in 1901, which probably found an appreciative marked in thirsty forge workers. The drink, now marketed as Irn-Bru, has gone from strength to strength. Irn-Bru outsells Coca Cola in Scotland and Barr themselves have been going global, becoming especially popular in Russia, which shares Scotland's sweet tooth. Barr employs 1,200, but moved its manufacturing capacity to Cumbernauld some years ago.

Parkhead is probably just too far from the centre and West End of Glasgow to share much in its reinvention as a city of culture, city of finance or city of lifestyle. Whatever one's thoughts on the Forge shopping centre, it has possibly saved Parkhead from the kind of decline seen in certain other areas of the city, for example in Possil. The works associated with the 2014 Commonwealth Games have also brought benefits to the area. Parkhead (with its satellites) is now an area with a semi-marginalised, low-skilled population, much declined from its height of 50,000 to about 15,000. It is hard to imagine the prosperity and skills base of a century ago returning to the area in the immediately foreseeable future. Indeed, it is more likely that a European trophy might return to Paradise.

CHAPTER FOURTEEN

Rutherglen Regained

'RU'GLEN'S WEE ROON reid lums reekin' briskly' do not do so within Glasgow City's boundaries. This despite the fact that the closest point in Rutherglen to George Square is less than a mile and a half as the crow flies. By contrast, you are still more than ten miles from Edinburgh on the M8 when a sign announces you are in that city. Glasgow's absurdly constricted boundaries are nowhere more apparent than with the case of Rutherglen. Insult is added to injury when it is recalled that historically Ru'glen was one of the Glasgow Burghs that sent an MP to Parliament before 1832. A previous local government reorganisation had given the town to Glasgow, only for it to be snatched back again in the mid-1990s – and given to South Lanarkshire, of which county it is one of the most northerly parts. The civic motto of the town was *Ex fumo fama*, which basically means 'Let the lums reek'.

Rutherglen is possibly older than Glasgow, with a good claim to be Scotland's first Royal burgh, its charter dating from David 1 in 1126. In the Middle Ages, Rutherglen was the head of River Clyde navigation and more commercially important than Glasgow. Around 1330, the town paid five per cent of all Scotland's burgh taxes.

With the growth of Glasgow, Rutherglen's importance declined, though in 1679 it was the scene of stirring historical events. A group of Covenanters rode into the town and at the Mercat Cross burnt various documents associated with Charles II and Episcopacy. And in the Declaration of Rutherglen, these early republicans declared the king overthrown. The insurgents had their success over Bloody Clavers (Bonnie Dundee) at the battle of Drumclog soon after. However, the Covenanters met their nemesis at Bothwell Brig later in the same year. These events form the backbone of Walter Scott's novel, *Old Mortality* (1816).

Ru'glens stagnation and decline was arrested and turned round by the industrialisation of the West of Scotland. In his *History of Rutherglen and East Kilbride* (1793), David Ure gave the number of its inhabitants as 1,630, adding 'the population, owing to the growth of manufactures, is on the increase'. Ru'glen was still mainly a weaving town, with 250 weavers and just 60 colliers, according to Ure. The

Rutherglen

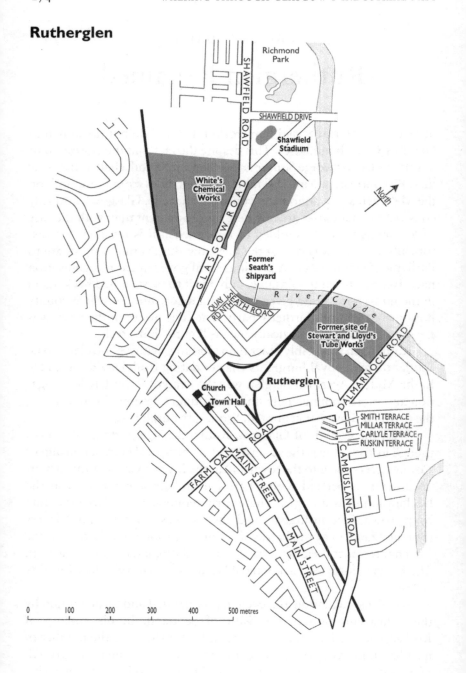

Rutherglen Route Summary

1 Take a train to Rutherglen station.

2 Gain Farmeloan Road and follow it to Cambuslang Road, where the Workmen's Terraces are located.

3 A further stravaig down Dalmarnock Road to the Clyde is an option, but retracing your steps is necessary.

4 Return to Main Street, which calls for careful attention, and from there the Glasgow Road takes you to Shawfield, past the sites of White's works.

5 A return to Ru'glen station can be made by an adventurous detour to Seath Road. This is not for the faint-hearted!

Approximate route time: 2.5 hours

discovery of large coal deposits in the area led to the sinking of mines and an account from the early 19th century stated that now Rutherglen 'was chiefly inhabited by coal hewers'. One of the mines, the Farme Colliery, built its own steam engine to drain the mine in 1810. The engine operated there till 1915, and is now in the Summerlee Industrial Museum in Coatbridge. Farmeloan Road and Farme Cross still today commemorate this pit. The Stonelaw mine was another. Soon the mines were followed by bleach fields and dyeworks, characteristic of the early textile phase of industrialisation, and then heavy industry arrived in turn.

In 1808, the Whites opened their Shawfield Chemical Works in Rutherglen. Shawfield closed in 1965 after a century and a half of infamy. The Whites ran the works here, and others factories in their empire, as a family company for over a century. The third White, John, was a Christian philanthropist, and a Free Kirker after the Disruption of 1843. This fine man gave generously to missions to Christianise the African heathen, and to the building of the Christian Institute in Glasgow's Bothwell Street. This fine man was a financial backer of the alcohol prohibition campaign, and also of the Glasgow Liberal Party, paying off the debts of the Liberal Club. This fine man, who conducted extensive family prayers every day, was given a peerage by Gladstone, and became Lord Overtoun, buying a 3,000-acre estate at Bowling on the Clyde. This fine man was a mass murderer.

The Shawfield works produced chrome – indeed, they were the largest producer in Britain, possibly the largest in the world for a while. At first chrome was used in the dyestuffs industry, but later the development of electro plating created an insatiable demand for the metal. The production of this commodity made the Shaws into multi-millionaires, yet their legacy continues to kill and maim. The untreated effluent of the works ran into the Mall's Mire burn and then into the Clyde. Even today, the level of chromium in the burn is 825 times the permitted amount. Chromium is highly carcinogenic. With one per cent of Scotland's population, Rutherglen and its neighbour Cambuslang have 25 per cent of all Scotland's children's leukemia cancers. Today. Not a century ago. These twin towns also suffer a high concentration of otherwise rare children's kidney tumors.

During their lifetime, it has been estimated that the Shawfield works dumped 275 million litres a year of toxic phenols and cyanides into the surrounding water table. The air the factory produced was virtually unbreathable. As well as having high incidence of cancers such as those of the nose and throat, White's workers suffered severe respiratory problems from fumes laced with cyanide. Locals called the men 'White's Canaries' after their skin colour, or simply 'White's Dead Men'. One historian writes that 'the works were a filthy place where men laboured for 12 hours a day under degrading and danger-ous conditions for mimimal wages'. These wages were four (old) pence an hour for labourers.

White would stand at the gates of the factory at the end of shifts and chastise workers upon leaving if they had flecks of chrome on their clothing or footwear, shouting, 'Hey, man, gang back and daud yer shin. Di ye no see ye're cairrying awa siller when ye cairry crum on yer bitts'. The work in this Inferno was largely unskilled and the labourers difficult to organise, but they took part in the upsurge of strikes known as the New Unionism, embracing the unskilled and semi-skilled workers, in the 1880s and 1890s. Just at the peak of his self-satisfied fame, when he had been knighted and was preparing the launch of a Christian Revivalist Crusade, White's Dead Men walked. They walked out of the factory in 1899 demanding a union and the right to be treated as human beings. The strike became a national issue, largely because the workers' case was taken up by Keir Hardie, after whom a street in Rutherglen is named.

Hardie wrote detailed articles in the *Labour Leader*, the newspaper of the Independent Labour Party, which exposed the conditions under which White exploited his men. These texts were made into a pamphlet, *White's Slaves: Lord Overtoun, Chrome, Charities and Cant*, and helped publicise their strike. But possibly the men relied too much on Hardie, and he soon had other fish to fry. With the formation of the Labour Party (LRC) in 1900, Hardie ceased to give White's his close attention. The men were forced back to work, having won minor concessions. The press and the middle-class political and church organisations of the day stood behind White, and his obituaries in newspapers in 1908 were sickening odes to his Christian integrity. An extracted example:

> A Christian of a noble type
> A man of God from youth
> A benefactor of the race
> A champion of the truth.

A Christian sabbatarian, White campaigned against the opening of the Glasgow People's Palace on a Sunday, the working man's only day off. Yet he ran his works seven days a week and sacked workers who failed to work Sundays. Only the *Glasgow Herald* mentioned the 'Overtoun Exposure' in its obituary, the rest of the press ignored it.

And still, a century later, the Ru'glen weans die.

Not all the pollution around Rutherglen was due to White's, though a 1990s estimate put the cost at cleaning up the Shawfield works alone at £20 million. These works are just one of the 27 dangerous sites in and around the town, possibly the highest concentration in the UK. One of these sites was the ground of Glencairn Park FC, where the terraces were built from industrial waste and were 26 times over the allowable limits for various pollutants. Another major polluter was the Clydebridge Steel works, opened in the 1880s in the river bend north of Rutherglen. This huge mill operated for more than a century before it was run down in the 1980s. There are still large polluted sites hereabouts, simply capped by a covering of earth. Others, similarly untreated, have been built over by housing and shops.

Anyway, let's cheer ourselves up and go walkabout. There may no longer be 'wee roon reid lums reekin in Ru'glen', but there is lots to see, exiting the train at Rutherglen station. Around here are some very fine red sandstone tenements, as there are at the south end of Farmeloan Road. Walk north to where it joins the Dalmarnock Road at Farme Cross, noting the excellent tenement standing at the north side of the cross. This was constructed in 1905 after a disastrous flood had destroyed the previous housing. Hereabouts is the old industrial centre of Rutherglen, which was replaced by trading and commercial estates built on the capped poisoned lands. Stewart and Lloyd's tube works lay to the west, and various chemical and engineering works were to the east. While this capping stopped airborne dust pollution, it did nothing to stop the chemicals leeching into the water table. The area now functions, as so often is case, a trading estate and a large supermarket. Not exactly where you would expect to find a Conservation Area, but there is one.

A small cluster of streets with the names of famous writers lies here. The Terraces of Smith, Millar, Carlyle and Ruskin commemorate eminent Scottish men of letters of the 18th and 19th centuries. These are neat cottage-style rows of houses, with small front and back gardens, recently restored and given protected status. A local resident playing fitba' with his son told me they had originally been miners' rows. On another occasion I was informed that they were cottages for workers in a formerly adjacent ropeworks. Actually there were built by the Glasgow Working Men's' Investment Trust and Building Society, between 1875 and 1882. This shows not only the admirable degree of self-help of the (skilled) workers involved in the enterprise but, in the names of the streets, their literary tastes as well.

I informed a local working his garden, who I got chatting to, that I was annexing Ru'glen to Glasgow and asked his opinion.

'I dinnae mind. I'm fae the Gorbals.' And he pointed out the not-faraway high Hutchesontown flats he had moved out of. 'And it might be a good idea. Sooth Lanarkshire's a wee bit slow getting things daen,' he added. Walking back up Farmeloan Road brings you to the town's Main Street.

Rutherglen was long a market town, having weekly markets as well as regular horse fairs, and this accounts for the width of the street and the breadth of the pavements, which were built for stalls. With the declining use of pit ponies and of horses on the land, the last fairs were held in 1900, I had read. However, the pavements of Main Street were busy with a farmer's market the last time I arrived, offering the local inhabitants the best of country produce, and maintaining the old Ru'glen traditions. Walking along the street gives a pleasant view on the north side. There is a solid post office and library, and a reconstruction of the former Mercat Cross, dating from 1926. Dominating all is the Town Hall, with its top-heavy tower, a prominent landmark from many surrounding vantage points. This was built in 1861 by Charles Wilson, and was the centre of burghal government till the mid-1970s. It is an attractive Scots Baronial revival building, and one of its features is the large collection of cast iron lions' heads on its western wall. It is undoubtedly Rutherglen's finest building – and was built by a Glasgow architect.

Just next to the town hall is Rutherglen's old parish church, set on a pre-Christian site; the original church dates from the late 12th century. The leafy graveyard is a delightful spot, almost like a country kirk, with its trees and fine collection of gravestones. The entrance arch to the kirkyard dates from the 1660s, and just inside are two sentry boxes, dated 1761, where the elders collected the offerings of the communicants. The present church was built in 1901, designed by another Glasgow architect, JJ Burnet, and replaced the one built in the 1790s, which itself had replaced the medieval foundation. Standing free in the kirkyard is a fine belltower, whose bell was forged in Holland in the 17th century. The tower is not 'Norman,' as stated by some observers. Though it has a northern French look about it, the tower was constructed in the later 15th century, and the gable of the demolished medieval kirk can still be seen on the western side of the tower.

Just past the kirk are the offices of the *Rutherglen Reformer*, the local paper, started in 1874 and still going strong on local loyalty. Rutherglen grew from about 2,000 people in 1800 to about 30,000 in 1900, and the population has remained remarkably stable since, falling only a little below this despite its industrial decline. Like many other districts around Glasgow, it is largely a dormitory for people who work in the city.

No longer here, though, is the Saracen Fountain, which was removed in 1900 to help traffic flow, and relocated in Overtoun Park to the south. The broad pavements of Ru'glen would seem wide enough to me to take the fountain, and its reinstatement here would add much to the look of Main Street. Turning south up Mill Street takes you to the park, which was a gift to the burgh in the will of White when he died in 1908. Overtoun Park lies in middle-class Rutherglen, with its terraces and villas. A pleasant area, though there are no significant buildings. But there is another possible walk from Main Street, slightly more on the wild side.

The Glasgow Road turns north towards the city, and taking it as far as and across the railway bridge, where Quay Road, passing under the new M74 motorway, leads you to yet another light industrial trading estate. My aim was to get to Seath Street, where Ru'glen's most surprising industry had been located. Masted ships were cut off from Rutherglen when the Glasgow burghers bridged the river. But the canny Ru'glonians developed a shipbuilding industry in the 1850s, building craft that could sail under the Clyde bridges; craft like the Cluthas, which were small cargo ships, or small paddle craft for pleasure uses. Of these, the *Lucy Ashton* used in England's Lake District was probably the most famous. The surprising place where this happened was Seath's yard, and it survived until after the First World War. I had seen the piles and quays of the yard from the Bridgeton side of the Clyde and set off to locate them for real.

Many dodgy dens of dereliction later I found the yard, or at least part of it that now hosts the local boat club. Here fanatics repair their craft, and launch them into the Clyde for trips down the river, through the weir at Glasgow Green, and onto the wide ocean. There was a great debate amongst the *cognoscenti* as to whether this was Seath's, or whether Ru'glen quay where the yard was located was a little upriver. But for the sake of historical continuity I am prepared to accept the present boat yard as the site. Getting to the other candidate for the honour would have involved climbing fences, dodging dogs and security guards, or even greater possible dangers.

From the Clyde, it is either back to the station, or along the Glasgow Road to verify the closeness of Glasgow and its Green to Ru'glen. This takes you past the still heavily polluted site of the White's chemical factories, which lay north of the present M74, and straddled both sides of the Glasgow Road, ground currently occupied by small trading or commercial units. Clyde Gateway was an organisation set up to regenerate the fabric of Glasgow's East End – and of Rutherglen, which I think makes for me a point I may have laboured in this chapter, with the further aim of raising the population of the area by 20,000 people. But even Clyde Gateway has struggled to fund the massive costs of a clean-up of poisoned sites, above all, of Shawfield.

Glasgow Road hereabouts is an avenue of footballing dreams. Glencairn FC's ground is on the left. The high level of poison in its construction materials didn't stop the 'Chookie Hens,' as they were nicknamed, winning the Scottish Junior Cup four times. Their stadium has been redeveloped as New Southcroft Park for the club and for wider social use as a valuable local facility. And further on is the former Shawfield stadium of Clyde FC. The 'Bully Wee,' as they were called, were founded in Rutherglen in 1898, and were twice Scottish Cup winners. The absurdity of Ru'glen's exclusion from Glasgow is shown by the fact that you could shoot in Ru'glen and score in Glasgow, since part of the pitch, the northern goalmouth area, fell within the city. That was until the latest local authority gerrymander, when Ru'glen was given the northern goalposts of Shawfield as well.

Clyde moved out of Rutherglen to Cumbernauld some time ago, though the stadium continues to host dog racing. Remodeled in the 1930s as an Art Deco stadium, Shawfield was Scotland's Highbury. But to see it now, this is hard to believe. Most of the Art Deco features have gone, replaced by corrugated iron, or have simply decayed like the once smart entrance. I was lucky enough to see Aberdeen play a couple of times at Shawfield in the late '70s and early '80s, when some of the stadium's faded glories were still in place. But already the Clyde support was down to a thousand or so, and the grass on the pitch needed cutting. Or maybe that was a tactic to help the Bully Wee. Anyway, the Dons won. There is some talk of Clyde moving back to Rutherglen.

Even before you cross the bridge from Shawfield to Glasgow Green – it is five minutes to the Green and 20 to George Square – you are in Glasgow. And so too should Ru'glen be. But there is another thing that needs changing. White has a statue in Glasgow, in Cathedral Square. If Ru'glen ever comes back, that should be removed.

CHAPTER FIFTEEN

Around Bridgeton Cross

I COULD WELL be in a small minority, but if I were condemned to spend eternity wandering around one part of Mungo's City, then it would probably be within a circle prescribed by a radius of a mile or so from Brigton Cross – or 'Bridgeton' as it is increasingly and annoyingly pronounced. Here one can find a Venetian palace, a Byzantine mausoleum, a Baroque church and an Art Deco hotel, as well as the ghosts of an industrial history second to nowhere. Indeed, it could be claimed that the Industrial Revolution was born in Brigton.

The territories hereabouts might seem at first infertile regions in which to seek the pleasures of urban walking. Certainly, this is an area which has had decidedly bad press, exceeded only possibly by that of the Gorbals. Those who know Glasgow from 'No Mean City'-type hearsay will associate Bridgeton with razor gangs, Billy Boy sectarianism and some of the worst housing in Europe. My namesake and fellow North-Easter James Leslie Mitchell (aka Lewis Grassic Gibbon) stated in the 1930s in *The Scottish Scene* that hereabouts were 'over a hundred and fifty thousand human beings living in such conditions as the most bitterly pressed primitive in Tierra del Feugo never envisaged'. An exaggeration, certainly, but containing a deal of truth, at a time when certain areas in Glasgow shared the population density of Calcutta. But I suspect that Mitchell/Gibbon, like many others, actually wrote about Bridgeton and its satellites without having taken much trouble to get to know the place.

One thing that would astonish Gibbon is that today the population of Glasgow's East End area is probably a quarter of the number he quoted. Whole parliamentary constituencies – including Camlachie and Bridgeton itself, which was the Red Clydesider and Independent Labour Party rebel James Maxton's seat – have disappeared. If John Knox were to re-inhabit his Edinburgh house today, he would recognise the Royal Mile easily after 500 years. But from the eyes in the back of his head (which he surely possesses) on his statue in the Glasgow Necropolis overlooking the greater Bridgeton district, Knox would scarcely recognise the place after only 50 years.

If one looks at John Hume's *Industrial Archeology of Glasgow*

(1974), or at any OS map up till about 1960, Bridgeton was home to so many factories that you wonder where the people were. Bridgeton at its height was even more industrial than Govan or Anderston, which possibly made it the most industrialised few square miles on the planet. Nowhere have the effects of Glasgow's industrial decline been as visible. Here started the ill-fated Glasgow East Area Renewal (GEAR) project in the 1970s, when swathes of purportedly substandard housing was cleared and attempts were made to attract new manufacturing industry to the area, to replace the large works which had closed down or were in decline. But the industrial closures continued. These included the Arrol Bridge and Crane Works in the mid-1980s, and Anderson Strathclyde Mining Machinery (formerly Mavor and Coulson), which folded with the closure of the mines in 1992 and the world-renowned Templeton's carpet factory. Many more proud names in Scottish industrial history disappeared at that time. Half a billion pounds certainly cleared the slums, but the new industries didn't come – and the people left. It was *Last Exit from Bridgeton*, to quote the title of James McKenna's book of memories of the area in the 1950s and '60s. The situation at that time was well described by William Barr in *Glasgwegiana* (1973):

> You are struck by the general scene of decay and neglect that pervades the area. Street after street of tall tenements stand empty, their shattered windows open and gaping to the sky. Broken glass lies in profusion on the streets... and the unchecked running water floods into the street... the engineering works, mills and factories have been closed down leaving Brigton with the appearance of a ghost town.

Let's go walkabout. Take the train to Bridgeton station and emerge into the light at Bridgeton Cross. If it is your first entry to Brigton, a visual delight immediately meets the eye. At the Cross itself is one of Glasgow's best ornamental cast iron productions, the 50 feet high Umbrella, complete with clock tower, originally built to shelter the unemployed in the depression of the 1870s. Unlike many public cast iron works in Glasgow, it was not produced at the Saracen Foundry in Possil, but by the Sun Foundry. The Umbrella has recently been completely restored as part of a £3 million upgrade of the public realm at the Cross, which has made an incredible difference to the look and feel of the place. The jewel in the local crown was the Olympia, initially a music hall, then a cinema, then a cash and carry, then a

Around Bridgeton Cross

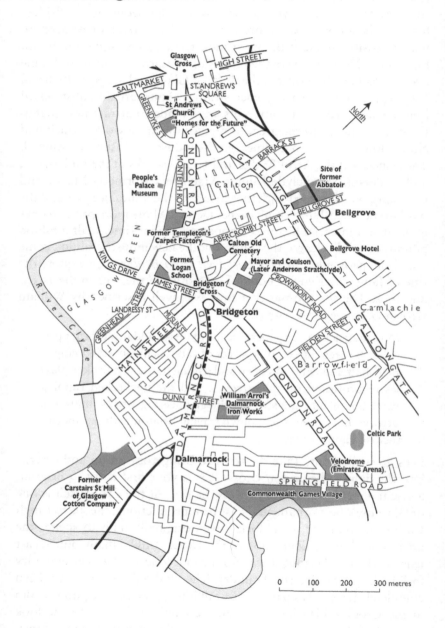

Around Bridgeton Cross Route Summaries

Route 1

1 Alight at Bridgeton station and walk from the Cross down James Street.

2 Head along Greenhead Street, admiring the tenements, then cross Main Street and proceed along Dunn Street and Poplin Street to Dalmarnock station.

3 Walk down to the Carstairs Cotton Mill, then swing east to cross Dalmarnock Road to follow Springfield Road to the various Commonwealth Games sites.

4 Trend back along the London Road until Dunn Street. Here, you can view the remains of Arrol's Dalmarnock Ironworks.

5 Return to Dalmarnock Road, then turn right and head back to the Cross.

6 Optional refreshments in the library café within the Olympia Building.

Approximate route time: 2.5 hours

Route 2

1 Begin at Bridgeton station and proceed down James Street.

2 Turn right past Logan's and McPhail's schools and walk on until you reach Templeton's building.

3 Regain the London Road, then go on to Abercromby Street to visit the Calton Old Cemetery.

4 Pass Bridgeton Business Centre and turn right into Crownpoint Road just before Bridgeton Health Centre. This is the heart of old industrial Bridgeton.

5 Continue until you emerge on Fielden Street. Opposite is the Barrowfield.

6 Head south down Fielden Street and turn right again at the London Road and back to the Cross past the Orange Lodge headquarters on the right.

Approximate route time: 2.5 hours

Route 3

1   Alight at Bellgrove station and walk down to the Gallowgate.

2   Head west past The Hielan Jessie and you will soon reach Bain Street.

3   Proceed further, past the Barras and Barrowland, towards Glasgow Cross.

4   Continue towards St Andrew's in the Square and consider stopping there for some delicious food.

5   Proceed to Greendyke Street and Homes for the Future (with an optional diversion to Charlotte Street) to the Green and the People's Palace, which has the Doulton Fountain outside.

6   Head along Menteith Row, with its horrendous '80s housing already falling into decay, until you see The Calton Bar.

7   Go across the London Road and into the innards of The Calton, eventually regaining the Gallowgate at the former City Abattoir.

8   Therafter, it is a short distance to Bellgrove station and douce Dennistoun.

Approximate route time: 3 hours

ruin – now fully restored as the local library and with workspace and sporting facilities. There are a number of striking tenement buildings at the Cross, traditionally the more affluent part of Brigton, and these would have been originally middle-class dwellings. The granite-pillared Trustee Savings Bank at 40–42 (now a betting office) and the blonde sandstone building with its fine oriel window at 32–38 are outstanding.

Here there are many other things of interest. In Landressy Street, next to the public library, stood till the mid-1980s the Bridgeton Working Men's Club. Clubs like this one, founded in 1865, though latterly becoming mainly drinking quarters, initially provided places of entertainment and instruction for the working man before 1914. The Bridgeton Club had a library of 2,000 volumes, mainly Victorian classics like Dickens, Scott and Burns, and took a selection of newspapers. But its main attraction would appear to have been the billiard hall, which raised half of the club's total income in 1902. In Bridgeton there was no more popular reading than the poems of Burns. The Bridgeton Burns Club, founded in 1870, became the largest in the

Bridgeton Working Men's Club: A representation of the now-demolished buildings where the club, founded in 1865, was based from 1899. It had an equally fine interior, and should have been renovated, not replaced by nondescript brick flats.

world, with 1,400 members, and it sponsored competitions in local schools for the recitation and singing of the Bard's works. Burns himself visited this area when it was still mainly a weaving suburb of Glasgow, staying at the Saracen's Head Inn in 1788 in nearby Calton. As part of the regeneration of the Cross, there has been erected a sandstone memorial to Burns, with the simple inscription 'LUV' on it. Landressy Street would appear to have been the cultural heart of Brigton, as it also contained the original local library, yet another of the fine series constructed by JR Rhind in 1905–6.

The finest tenements, and those which escaped demolition, are the cluster around the Cross, as indeed is the case with other areas, such as Govan. Elsewhere, almost all of Brigton's 19th-century working-class tenement housing has been demolished. People tend to think that the Glasgow tenements were always there, emerging as if from some prehistoric eruption. But till the 1870s and 1880s much of the city – even in the industrial, working-class areas – was still composed of lower terraced housing, detached houses or cottages, almost none of which now survive.

There is a wonderful painting by John Quinton Pringle called *Muslin Street, Bridgeton*, executed in the 1880s. (This is in Edinburgh City Art Galleries, which fact I regard as an affront to this city.) At this time Bridgeton, annexed by Glasgow in 1846, was still mainly a textile producing area, though heavy industry was moving in. Its population had grown from about 4,000 in 1800 to 64,000 – and was still growing. A brass founder's with its ventilation slats is depicted in Pringle's painting of Muslin Street. Pringle shows us Bridgeton from the roof of his house, and we see one three-storey tenement, but mainly two-storey, white harled and red pantile roofed housing, with the lums of the cotton mills in the background. Pringle, a highly skilled artisan (he was an optical repairer) was self-taught, and for me his superiority over his contemporary Glasgow Boys is undisputed. As one heads southwards from Bridgeton Cross down Main Street, the adjoining Mill Street, Poplin Street and Muslin Street (and Dale Street) remind you that before heavy engineering this was cotton country, and hereabout lie the gaunt ruins of former mills, such as the huge Carstairs Street Cotton Mill, which once employed 4,000 workers, and is now storage units. As spinning was mechanised, domestic spinning declined and the trade moved into factories, many of which were in the East End. Bridgeton was a centre of the cotton–spinners' strike in the 1830s, the details of which are given in the chapter on Anderston. At first, mechanised spinning increased the number of handloom weavers, but that trade too was soon mechanised and weaving, like spinning, transferred largely to factory production. In the process, weaving became in large part a female occupation. Though difficult to organise in trade unions, the women were quick to take industrial action. In 1863, 1875 and again in 1885, female mill hands struck work in Brigton's mills against wage reductions.

Almost totally cleared of its tenements in the '60s and '70s, the area south from Brigton Cross to Dunn Street is now almost entirely re-populated with a wide variety (and quality) of new housing. The area further southwards, better known as Dalmarnock, was similarly cleared of people (many moving to Brigton proper across Dunn Street) and factories, but – apart from a large number of show and travelling people in riverside sites – it is still largely derelict. The fine yet no longer educationally used Strathclyde School, beside the Carstairs Mill, is testimony to the population that once lived hereabouts. The refurbishment of the Dalmarnock station (once the second least-used in the UK!) and the construction of the Commonwealth Games Village on the eastern edge of Dalmarnock on London Road is hopefully breathing new life into the area. The Village was originally designated to be for social housing after games were over, but now the policy has become that of selling most of the houses off, with social housing representing a minority of the homes. A missed opportunity. The Velodrome, currently designated Emirates Arena, a major centre for the Games, has also been built on waste ground at the Springfield Road, hopefully clustering other developments round it.

Dalmarnock is now mainly wasteland, with odd pockets of housing, sliced through by a new dual carriageway linking the M8 to the M74. (This road's purpose was in part to make the homes at the Games Village more sellable, and construction involved the demolition of good quality tenements in Ardelea Street and Springfield Road). Signs of regeneration are yet few, in the land of dookits and back alley boxing clubs. Yet Dalmarnock was once booming, the site of many industries, including one only second in the East End to Beardmore's in Parkhead, the Dalmarnock Iron Works. These were established by William Arrol in the 1870s, at a huge site with its own railway sidings, between Dunn Street and Nuneaton Street, and they continued in operation till the mid-1980s. A part of the former Arrol building can still be seen on the eastern side of Dunn Street. Here up to 5,000 men earned their bread.

Arrol was Scotland's greatest engineer since Telford. The firm made cranes, such as the world-famous Titan cranes, which are now protected monuments where they survive, from Clydebank to Nagasaki, but Arrol was mainly a structural engineer, and himself built many of the factories of Glasgow's heavy industrial period. Arrol's main memorial is, however, the Forth Rail Bridge, a marvel of beauty as well as of engineering, though we should remember the 100 men killed in its construction. Arrol also constructed the replacement Tay Rail Bridge, as well as London's Tower Bridge. These fine bridges all endure, but what remains in Dalmarnock? One thing that no longer does is Stoddart's Bedding Factory. I came here as a young married man in the 1970s to buy a bed requested that it be delivered to my address. Being asked where that was, I though the best response would be to mention a location known throughout the western world. 'Near Partick,' I said. 'Is that in Glasgow?' was the salesperson's reply. Possibly in the hard time that followed, the sales rep's limited geographical knowledge did not help the firm's survival.

The mention of Dalmarnock raises an interesting question, i.e. that of the Brigtons of the Mind. In my innocence, I had taken Brigton to be the postal district (as the parliamentary constituency has gone) of G40. Many years of walking about the area, talking to locals and giving talks in and about Brigton has convinced me of the error of my ways. Dalmarnockonians would probably agree to being in Brigton as long as the area's sub-divisional status was recognised. As we shall see, other areas of G40 would take to the barricades at the very suggestion that they were parts of Greater Brigton. Hence the carefully chosen title of this chapter, Around Brigton Cross.

East of Fielden Street and south of the Gallowgate, but north of the London Road, is an area that once was part of the Barrowfield estate, and used to be the site of a housing estate called Barrowfield that was featured in documentaries about social deprivation in the '70s and '80s. The inter-war estate that stood there has been totally demolished and replaced by good quality, low-density housing. The area appears also to have undergone a name change and now tends to be called Camlachie. There is an actual Camlachie Street just south of the Gallowgate, but historical Camlachie really lay where the Forge Retail Park now squats to the north. If this area is Brigton improper, then so too is the area to the north of the Gallowgate as one trends westwards, which I have heard referred to as Bellgrove after the railway station and the Bellgrove Hotel, or Whitevale after the still-standing (as of 2015) but vacant baths and steamie here. The Art Deco Bellgrove Hotel was constructed for the 1938 Empire Exhibition, but has mainly been run subsequently as a Model Lodging House. Lying on one of the main linear routes to the Commonwealth Games site, it benefitted from a major exterior face-lift in 2014. Reports of the state of the interior, and of the facilities for its residents, are not so encouraging however, and improvements have been demanded by the City Council.

Clifford Hanley, who penned 'Scotland the Brave', was also author of the autobiography, *Dancing in the Streets* (1984), and he spent his first six years hereabouts. He was aware, or maybe had a maw that was aware, of fine social differentiations; the importance of being, literally, on the right side of the tracks. South from the Gallowgate towards Bridgeton Cross was dangerous, while north towards Dennistoun was safer, as he comments:

> South of Gallowgate meant Cubie Street and Soho Street, and I never went down Soho Street. It was always north that our wanderings took us, the north separated from Gallowgate by the railway.

And south of the Gallowgate, from Fielden Street to Abercromby Street, is definitely Bridgeton. Continuing west you pass on that south side St Mungo's Academy, renovated under the controversial Schools

2002 Private Public Partnership scheme, and beyond which lay a concentration of engineering and textile works around Crownpoint Road and Broad Street, including the Mavor and Coulson works. This was set up in the 1890s and was an advanced electrical engineering works. It installed Glasgow's first electric street lighting and it also provided the mechanised cutting machinery for much of the Scottish coalfield, as well as pioneering electrical ship propulsion technology. Always a great equipment supplier to the Soviet Union, Mavor and Coulson's successor, Anderson Strathclyde, suffered badly from that country's collapse as well as from Thatcher's butchery of the UK coal industry after the 1984 miners' strike, and the firm closed its doors in the 1990s after a century of technological pioneering. The achievements of its founder, Henry Mavor, are little remembered, and he is mainly known today as the father of James Bridie, the playwright and founder of the Citizens Theatre.

Further westwards, on the 'Bellgrove' side, is the former meat and cattle market, one of Glasgow's many 19th-century civic markets, whose façade has been lovingly retained, though the market is no longer used. Aside from the stunning façade there are many things around here to look at. At the back end of Graham Square is the 18th-century inn (now housing) where the cattle dealers and drovers would reside during sales, while, outside, shawlie women would queue for pails of blood with which to make black puddings and combat anemia in their weans. While much of the huge site of the market remains sadly derelict and littered, 30 years after its closure, Graham Square hosts a development of housing association properties of the highest social and architectural merit, which won a Saltire Award in 2001.

Mavor and Coulson advert: Pioneers in electrical engineering, Mavor and Coulson were well placed to profit from the development of new weapons such as tanks and armoured cars that were brought in during the First World War.

A walk up Bellgrove Street takes you to Duke Street. Turning west you soon pass below the Glasgow Necropolis. Though technically outwith Bridgeton, Glasgow's graveyard for its wealthy citizens is well worth a visit, especially now that it has been largely restored. Below it is found probably the only large-scale factory left in this area: the Tennent's Brewery, which, incidentally, must also be the oldest industrial undertaking in the city, dating from 1556. In the Necropolis are Gothic tombs and Byzantine-style mausoleums, some of which are bigger than the average single-end that most people in and around Bridgeton once inhabited. But that there were better-class tenements here is shown by the rosy sandstone survival on Hunter Street, opposite the Tennent's Brewery, a fine building with elaborate bas-reliefs of the brewing trade. It has to be admitted, though, that not many of the buildings in this area were of this standard, and few of the Victorian and Edwardian tenements remain. Heading south again from Tennent's brewery by Barrack Street (so called because troops were stationed there from its construction in 1795 as a counter measure to local radicalism) takes you back to the Gallowgate.

Returning to this point of the Gallowgate, you are no longer in Bridgeton. Definitely. Once past Abercromby Street and across the Gallowgate, you are in The Calton, an area bounded by the triangle of Abercromby Street, the Gallowgate and the London Road. Abercromby Street, running from the Gallowgate to the London Road, is the Front Line between Brigton and Calton, or possibly a disputed No-Mans' Land, as St Mary's RC Church, where Celtic were formed in 1888, though a Caltonian outpost, is on the Brigton side, as too is the Old Calton Graveyard – but between them lies the Bridgeton Health Centre.

Further west, on the south side of the Gallowgate where Claythorn Street meets it, are two fabulously restored 18th-century tenements, one with the Hielan Jessie pub occupying its lower floor. But most of The Calton consisted of poor 19th-century tenements, very few of which are left. Like The Garngad and The Gorbals, The Calton in the 19th century was an area mainly inhabited by unskilled Irish immigrants, who took low skilled, low-paid work and occupied low-quality and overcrowded housing. Even today, The Calton is one of the poorest areas of Glasgow, much more so than neighbouring Brigton, for example. Some good quality social housing is being constructed here, but there is still a way to go, as a walkabout in the interior between the three arterial roads will show. Here as well as boarded-up, closed former schools we have the interesting one-time Eastern District Police Buildings with Italianate touches, another design by John Carrick, the city architect from 1862–89 and a much underrated figure. But not everything is crumbling away.

In a bold move, a former clay pipe factory and subsequent warehouse in Bain Street has been converted into flats, in the middle to lower price range, showing that regeneration is slowly reaching the more obscure corners of the city. Next you pass the world-famous Barrowland Ballroom to reach the Barras themselves, the centre of reset goods, hucksters, conmen – and the odd bargain. In the narrow streets around here, you could almost believe yourself in the Third World. Here also can be found the Saracen Head Inn, built in 1754, where the old stagecoach used to depart for its 12-day journey to London (or the Sarry Heid, as it is locally known – even Sorry Heid by hangover sufferers). Wordsworth – as well as Johnson and Boswell – visited here at the time when it was the rendezvous of the town's elite. A huge five-gallon punch bowl from the Sarry Heid, now in the People's Palace, commemorates the drinking bouts of those days. The present Sarry Heid is on the site on the original, but in a late 19th-century tenement building.

Apart from the Sarry Heid itself, the most unobservant cannot fail to notice that almost all of the many drinking dens in this area sport iconography relating to Celtic Football Club and to Irish nationalism. Around Brigton Cross, the same pattern will be seen, but this time relating to Rangers FC and Ulster Unionism. The battles of three centuries ago have their historical interest, but their residue has no place in Glasgow today, and especially has no place in public houses, which gain licenses to serve the public, not to operate as private drinking clubs for tribal allegiates. It is unfortunate that the city authorities are hesitant to tackle this issue head on by withdrawing licenses from all public houses which are not such, i.e. open to the general public. Even as an Aberdeen supporter, or as a simple passer-by, I would hesitate to enter any of these resorts.

At Glasgow Cross we come to the magnificent Tolbooth Steeple, the finest in Scotland, which survived plans by the council in the '60s and '70s to remove it and replace it with a traffic roundabout, and we come also to the limits of The Calton, and turn our steps back eastwards towards Brigton – though by a detour through an area that is as rich in historical and built legacy as any in the entire city. St Andrew's Square could be the surprise of your day if you don't know the city.

A recent housing development in traditional 18th-century style flanks the St Andrew's Church, one of the gems of Glasgow's ecclesiastic architecture, and now an arts centre and the Café Source restaurant. The church, finished in 1757, was modeled on St Martin in the Fields in London to a design by Dreghorn and boasts magnificent plasterwork inside. It is undoubtedly one of the finest baroque churches in Britain. Just south on the corner of Greendyke Street is the Kirk of St Andrew's by the Green, known as the Whistlin Kirk or the Piskie Kirk, finished seven years earlier. Apparently the first Episcopalian place of worship to be built in the city after 1689, the mason who built it was excommunicated by the Glasgow Presbytery. The fact that the Kirk had an organ gave it its name. Again, imaginative thinking has restored it as Glasgow Association of Mental Health offices, and the graveyard has also been renovated. The existence of such prestigious kirks here reminds us that, unlike other industrial areas of Glasgow such as Govan or Springburn, the East End developed beside, and then overwhelmed, an area inhabited by the upper echelons of the Dear Green Place. The University in the High Street itself backed onto this area, till its scholars fled to the West End in the 1870s.

The Whistlin Kirk (as well as a pub of that name) faces Glasgow Green itself. A stone's throw from the Green was Paddy's Market, where the poorest came to buy things that most of us would be embarrassed to give away. As far back as the 1870s, Tweed, in his *Guide to Glasgow and the Clyde*, observed:

> ... a low wooden erection, sacred to the vending of old clothes, known as Paddy's Market. It is unsightly in its appearance, unpleasant in its associations, and it is to be hoped it will soon be removed.

Tweed would be pleased to know that Glasgow Council has finally succeeded in closing down Paddy's, allegedly because of its criminal connections, but more likely as a part of the social cleansing of the area.

Throw the stone the other way from here towards Greendyke Street and we have the Homes for the Future, staggeringly effective models for urban living built for Glasgow's year as UK City of Architecture and Design in 1999 – and snapped up despite the six-figure price tags, showing that many people want to live city centre. And why ever not? The view over the Green and the Clyde from these houses, to the Cathkin Braes in the far south, is worth a mortgage itself. These new houses are amongst the best of contemporary Scottish architecture and fit well with the 1960s school next to them, designed by Glasgow architect Coia, one of the few structures worth preserving from that period. This was initially a Catholic girls' secondary school and is a fine building, showing that not all '60s architecture was bad; it is no longer a school, but offices.

The Green is also a salutary reminder of many of the good things about the old East End. It was here that the early trade unions held their demonstrations, from the striking Calton Weavers in 1787 to the UCS work-in in the 1970s. This was also where the suffragettes and temperance fighters staged their rallies, and where those opposed to the slaughter of the First World War bravely made their case. The Weavers' Strike of 1787 was the first major industrial dispute in Glasgow's – or Scotland's – history. The cloth masters cut the price for the goods they put out to the weavers, and in and around Glasgow they struck work. When the weavers organised a demonstration, the soldiers were called out, fired on the demonstration in the Drygate, and six weavers killed, though only three of their names are known. They were John Page, Alexander Millar and James Ainsley. These first martyrs of the Scottish working class were buried in the Old Calton Graveyard in Abercrombie Street, after a funeral attended by 6,000 people. A commemorative plaque recalls the events, explicitly denouncing their 'martyrdom' by the civic authorities. Only one name is still legible, that of Page. In this graveyard, too, lies the Rev James Smith, who was Abraham Lincoln's minister, and later US consul in Scotland.

Despite the setback, the weavers hereabouts were apparently not cowed. Alexander Allan, one of the weaving capitalists, built himself a mansion by the Clyde. Unlike his fellow weaving capitalist, Harvie (see the account of Harvie's Dyke in the Parkhead chapter), Allan did not block off the riverside right of way. Instead he had it built over, extending his gardens to the Clyde, but forcing walkers to pass through the tunnel that he constructed over the path, known as Allan's Pen. Outraged by this interference with their traditional access to the river, the weavers refused to accept work from Allan, even when he promised increased wages. Deeply troubled financially, Allan fled to Ireland, as Harvie was also to do. A Clyde flood swept most of the Pen away. Working people liked walking as a recreation and resented any interference with their rights.

It is interesting that the first local guide to walking was written in Bridgeton, by Hugh MacDonald in 1854. His *Rambles Round Glasgow* took MacDonald to many interesting places and for 50 years his was the main walking guide to the Glasgow area. MacDonald had been born in Bridgeton in 1817, one of 11 children, as was apprenticed as a calico block maker in the textile industry. He worked in the Barrowfield works, where children were employed in the bleachfield for 18 pence a day. MacDonald was politically active and contributed to Chartist publications, later breaking into publishing as a contributor to the *Glasgow Citizen* newspaper, where many of his walks were published. He deserves to be better known, and should be, now that a gate on the redeveloped Green has been named after him and the memorial erected to him has been placed in a prominent position behind the People's Palace.

MacDonald was especially attached to Glasgow Green and worried about the survival of its trees, since, 'The Orient blasts come laden with death from the Bridgeton factories.' He was familiar with the local right of way battles of Harvie's Dyke and Alan's Pen, and proud of the Green's political role:

> To the achievement of the great moral victory of 1832 (for in its fruits, which are not yet all reaped, it has indeed been great), the magnificent meetings on Glasgow Green must have contributed in no little degree.

The Green's role in political protest continued afterwards. In 1838, a huge demonstration took place on Glasgow Green in support of the People's Charter, which advocated universal male suffrage. Seventy trade unions with banners took part. The Glasgow Universal Suffrage Association was a moderate group, on the moral force wing of Chartism. It faded away after 1842, its remaining members turning to campaigns for teetotalism and to the formation of Chartist Churches, of which one was established in Bridgeton. But Chartism was revived in the hungry year of 1848, inspired by the Revolution in France, and in Bridgeton the barricades went up.

In February that year, a crowd gathered on the Green and demanded a minimum wage of two shillings a day; the city magistrates offered soup tickets instead. Later the crowd tore down the iron railings of Monteith Row and sacked shops for food and arms, advancing on the city centre. One eye-witness recalled later:

> In the year of 1848 I witnessed a procession of a large body of ill-fed, ill-clad and half armed Chartists, men women and boys, enter Buchanan Street. The procession turned sharp down the street and when passing Gordon Street fired two shots in the air.

Another states:

> This outbreak soon assumed an alarming aspect. The mob had
> rapidly increased, and shops were entered and robbed by the
> hungry people. A gunsmith in Exchange Square was entered and
> guns and ammunition carried off.

Police, troops and special constables charged the rioters and drove them
from the High Street and Saltmarket, arresting 150. The next day,
soldiers parading through Bridgeton were attacked and a barricade
was thrown up across the Gallowgate. This was assaulted by troops
and broken down, and after a subsequent series of exchanges of fire
at Main Street in Bridgeton, six demonstrators were shot and an
unspecified number killed. Two alleged ringleaders of the troubles,
Smith and Crosson, were summarily tried and given ten and 18 years'
transportation by Sheriff Allison (J Campbell, *Recollections of
Radical Times*, 1880).

The Green was always a demotic place, the population originally
having the right to dry their clothes and graze their animals on it, and
later the Glasgow Fair spilled onto the Green from the 1840s. The
song 'The Sports o' Glasgow Green' tells of Jocky and Jenny spending
a day at the fair:

> There were spinners, and clippers and darners
> Some rogues and some decent folk
> The chiels were a' merrily playing
> At prick the loop, dice and black jock.

Punch and Judy shows, exhibitions of dwarfs with a giant 'frae the
Kingdom o Fife' and a menagerie are all part of the fun till they repair
Lucky McNee's in Clyde Street. Then:

> Forfauchten wi drinking and dancing
> The twa they cam toddlin haim
> Wi rugging and riving and drawing
> They baith were wearied and lame.

Another song, 'Bonnie Glasgow Green,' tells the most improper story
of a lad, from Aberdeen I regret to say, who steals away the affections
of a girl spreading her clothes on the Green. Despite the fact that she is
engaged to a local mason, 'my Jamie that hews the stane/Tae mak oor
toon look braw,' the girl goes off with the Aberdonian. I have never
found the local women as accommodating.

Generations of tanner ba' football enthusiasts honed their skills
there. The Green was the first home of Rangers FC, and even today
Bridgeton and Rangers are held, shall we say, to have a certain special
relationship. It is fitting that Glasgow's People's Palace, a museum to
its rich working-class life is located there, and that a major renewal
programme has prepared the Green for the 21st century, supported by
Heritage Lottery and Scottish National Heritage funding. Central to
this was the restoration of the Doulton Fountain from the Empire
Exhibition of 1888, repaired and relocated outside the Palace. Described
as 'an exuberant terracotta wedding cake,' it celebrates an Empire at
its apogee; that a bolt of lightning shattered Victoria at its summit in
1894 was possibly a reminder that nothing lasts forever. It is the largest
terracotta sculpture in the world.

Glasgow's East End has traditionally put its best face to the Green,
with the now-vanished Monteith Row being originally composed of
grand town houses; these later were converted into slum warrens and
are now all gone, apart from one building which houses a 'hotel,'
often, as in this case, a euphemism hereabouts for a lodging house.
Another prestige address was Charlotte Street, where town mansions
housed entrepreneurs such as David Dale, one of the founders of
Glasgow's cotton industry. One house in this street, built in 1782, has
thankfully been saved by conversion into modern dwellings, winning
another Saltire Award in 1990. Dale's dwelling, which would have been
very similar, was demolished to make way for a car park. JG Lockhart,
Walter Scott's son-in-law and biographer, died in Charlotte Street,
while John Stuart Blackie, the eminent Greek scholar, was born there.

At the eastern end of the Green there is another example of this
area's rich built legacy, one of the world's most amazing factories –
Templeton's carpet factory, now, like so many of the industries of the
past, closed. William Leiper's 1889 design, based on the Doge's Palace
in Venice, and faced in polychrome brick, overcame the initial resist-
ance of the Council to having a factory on the Green itself, and the City
Council duly purchased its carpets from Templeton's for decades.
What is less well known is that a fault in design led to the collapse of
the façade, killing 29 female workers, and it had to be rebuilt. The
factory has escaped demolition by being converted into a restaurant
and brewery, as well as offices and smaller workspaces, and partly into
flatted dwellings. None in the world could have a finer façade. An idea
of the wealth amassed by many of Glasgow's industrialists before the
First World War can be seen in the fact that John Templeton, when he

died in 1918, left the equivalent in today's terms of a fortune of £275 million, the firm regularly earning profit rates of 15 per cent per annum. But even he was poor compared to Arrol, whose personal wealth on his death in 1913 amounted, in today's values, to almost £320 million.

A short distance east of Templeton's on McPhail Street is the former Greenview School, a splendid building, originally the mansion of the cotton baron McPhail, and dating from 1846. Its architect was Charles Wilson, probably Glasgow's best from the mid-19th century. The philanthropist James Buchanan left £30,000 for its conversion into a school 'for the maintenance and instruction of destitute children'. The year after the Education Act of 1872, which made education compulsory, the delightful 'Young Scholar in Studious Pose' was carved in sandstone by William Brodie and placed atop the building. The adjacent Logan and Johnstone School of Domestic Economy, which a beehive bas-relief, tells us was 'Instituted in 1890,' provided instruction for generations of Bridgeton girls, as an alternative to factory work. But both have long been surplus to their original requirements. They have each been converted into (not inexpensive) flatted dwellings, helping to bring new life to old buildings, and similarly reversing the area's depopulation. Interestingly, a new middle-class population is beginning to occupy the frontages to the Green, replicating the situation of over a century ago.

A pleasant continuation to the Rutherglen Bridge brings the Green to an end. Here at Flesher's Haugh could be found for many years a headless statue of James Watt, whose epoch-making discoveries regarding the development of a separate condenser for the steam engine came to him while walking hereabouts. It was this invention that allowed industry to move into towns from the water-powered countryside, and laid the basis for the industrialisation of Glasgow – and the wider world. The statue formerly decorated the entrance to the Atlantic Mills in Bridgeton and it has now been recapitated and placed safely outside the People's Palace, as one of the many statues of Watt in Glasgow. Main Street takes the explorer back to Brigton Cross.

The weaving period left its legacy of song. Many will have heard the words of the 'Calton Weaver,' which was written here. The author tells us:

Ah'm a weaver, a Calton weaver,
Ah'm a rash and a rovin blade,

I've got siller in ma pooches,
I'll gae follae the rovin trade.

But after an encounter with drink (Nancy Whisky), he repents:

Ah'l gae back tae the Calton weavin,
Ah'l fairly mak the shuttles fly,
For ah'l mak mair at the Calton weavin,
Than ever I did in a rovin wye.

Although possibly Glasgow's most famous weaver-poet, William Millar,
who wrote 'Wee Willie Winkie,' as well as other verse, was from
Dennistoun. Not so many know that Alex 'Sandy' Rodger, another
poetical weaver, wrote 'The Muckin o' Geordie's Byre' in Bridgeton.
Rodger was a Radical who was jailed more than once for illegal and
'seditious' writings and publications. He wrote a lampoon on George
IV's visit to Scotland in 1822, which mocked Walter Scott's panegyric
for the occasion, and Sandy's song's refrain, 'Wattie, noo the King's
come' had as its next line a suggestion as to where the Abbotsford
Wizard might place a kiss on the royal personage's anatomy. Rodger
took place in the assault on Harvie's Dyke (see *Paradise Lost* chapter),
and was shot at during the mêlée from within Harvie's mansion. This
weaver-poet heritage shows that Brigton's musical traditions are not
only those of Billy-Boy doggerel.

But it is impossible to ignore this in Bridgeton, with the Scottish
headquarters of the Orange Lodge situated just next to the Olympia at
the Cross. When my fellow Aberdonian, Paton, came to Glasgow in the
early 20th century, he lived in Bridgeton for a while and commented
on the sectarianism he found here in his fascinating autobiography,
Proletarian Pilgrimage (1935). As a socialist, he initially 'watched this
faction fight with a pitying contempt for both sides,' until the Orangemen began to cause trouble at the ILP meetings at Bridgeton Cross.
Unlike in Partick, where this turned violent, Paton observed of the
Orangemen that, '… in Bridgeton, their opposition, although a nuisance, never went beyond noisy interruption'. After 1918, Orangeism
in Bridgeton degenerated into lumpen proletarian criminality and
gang warfare, wonderfully depicted in Edwin Morgan's poem 'King
Billy,' on the death of a gang leader.

Go from the grave. The shrill flutes
Are silent, the march dispersed.
Deplore what is to be deplored,
And then find out the rest.

Before the war, Paton tells us in *Proletarian Pilgrimage*, the Bridgeton ILP were a small group of about 40 people; in 1922 James Maxton won Bridgeton for the ILP with about 60 per cent of the vote. And it was a protest at housing conditions as much, if not more, than industrial exploitation, which swept Maxton to power. This issue gained especial importance with the winning of the vote in 1918 by a large sector of the female population, and housing was an issue on which Maxton fought hard. Maxton was not from Bridgeton, but he taught in Green Street School in The Calton, which was part of the parliamentary constituency that he represented in Westminster from 1922 till his death in 1946. They used to say they weighed, not counted, his votes, and he was revered and loved by the local population. In the 1930s the Unionists, as the Tories then called themselves, stood no less a person than the Grand Master of the Orange Lodge in Scotland against Maxton, but Maxton still won.

Calton's songwriting traditions continued with the works of the late Matt McGinn. He was an activist in the Communist party, which he later left, and wrote songs in support of many working-class struggles, such as the UCS work-in. One of the songs he wrote actually takes its inspiration from a weavers' refrain, though 'If it Wisnae for the Weavers' is from Forfarshire, not Calton. In the affluent '60s, McGinn reminded his fellow workers of their past struggles:

Too ra loo ra loo ra loo
I'll tell ye something awfu' true
Ye wouldnae hae yer telly the noo
If it wisnae for the Unions.

Before going to Ruskin College and becoming a teacher, McGinn worked in various places on Clydeside, including the GKN factory in Hillington. This was reputedly 'the noisiest factory in Britain' and McGinn had only been there two days when he initiated a strike.

The East End may never become a major tourist destination, but in a couple of miles radius from Bridgeton Cross, there is more to see and think on than in many, indeed any, of the more salubrious areas of Glasgow. Being located so close to the city's thriving centre, with its expanding commercial and cultural activities and increased demand for housing, Bridgeton is possibly better placed than many other post-industrial areas to benefit from Glasgow's attempted re-invention of itself as a city of the future, though one building firmly on its past. In the last decade there have been more positive developments in the built fabric of the area we have wandered through than possibly any other in this book, the Gorbals aside. But, improvements notwith-standing, real problems remain. The good jobs in the post-industrial city are not ones for which most of Bridgeton's residents are qualified. And we cannot forget that Bridgeton lies within that Glasgow which is still the cancer and heart attack capital of Europe. But walking around its streets does not cause me despair. There is room for optimism if the motto of the Bridgeton Working Men's Club is heeded:

Learn from the Past,
Use well the Future.

Some other books published by **LUATH** PRESS

A Glasgow Mosaic: Cultural Icons of the City
Ian R Mitchell
ISBN: 978-1-908373-66-3 PBK £9.99

A Glasgow Mosaic presents a broad view of Glasgow's industrial, social and intellectual history. From public art to socialist memorials, and from factories to cultural hubs, Ian R Mitchell takes the reader on a guided tour of Glasgow, outlining walking routes which encompass the city's forgotten icons.

Mountain Days and Bothy Nights
Dave Brown & Ian R Mitchell
ISBN: 978-1-906307-83-7 PBK £7.50

This classic bothy book is a celebration of hillwalking – the people who do it, the stories they tell and the places they sleep, the legendary walkers, the mountain craftsmen and the Goretex and gaiters brigade – and the best and the worst of the dosses, howffs and bothies of the Scottish hills.

Clydeside: Red, Orange and Green
Ian R Mitchell
ISBN: 978-1-906307-70-7 PBK £9.99

Ian R Mitchell takes the reader on an urban promenade along the Clyde, telling stories of conflicts, people and communities. Exploring more than just Glasgow itself, Mitchell reveals the unseen side of the diverse towns and villages along the Clyde.

Walking through Scotland's History: Two Thousand Years on Foot
Ian R Mitchell
ISBN: 978-1-905222-44-5 PBK £7.99

Walking through Scotland's History leads the way on a tour of the missionaries, mapmakers and military leaders who have trodden Scottish paths over the last 2,000 years. Ian R Mitchell examines the lives of the drovers, distillers, fishwives and workers for whom walking was a means of survival.

Details of these and other books published by Luath Press can be found at: **www.luath.co.uk**

Luath Press Limited

committed to publishing well written books worth reading

LUATH PRESS takes its name from Robert Burns, whose little collie Luath (*Gael.*, swift or nimble) tripped up Jean Armour at a wedding and gave him the chance to speak to the woman who was to be his wife and the abiding love of his life. Burns called one of 'The Twa Dogs' Luath after Cuchullin's hunting dog in Ossian's *Fingal*. Luath Press was established in 1981 in the heart of Burns country, and now resides a few steps up the road from Burns' first lodgings on Edinburgh's Royal Mile. Luath offers you distinctive writing with a hint of unexpected pleasures.

Most bookshops in the UK, the US, Canada, Australia, New Zealand and parts of Europe either carry our books in stock or can order them for you. To order direct from us, please send a £sterling cheque, postal order, international money order or your credit card details (number, address of cardholder and expiry date) to us at the address below. Please add post and packing as follows: UK – £1.00 per delivery address; overseas surface mail – £2.50 per delivery address; overseas airmail – £3.50 for the first book to each delivery address, plus £1.00 for each additional book by airmail to the same address. If your order is a gift, we will happily enclose your card or message at no extra charge.

Luath Press Limited
543/2 Castlehill
The Royal Mile
Edinburgh EH1 2ND
Scotland

Telephone: 0131 225 4326 (24 hours)
email: sales@luath.co.uk
Website: www.luath.co.uk